Reading 2

without answers

Liz Driscoll

CAMBRIDGE
UNIVERSITY PRESS

CAMBRIDGE UNIVERSITY PRESS
Cambridge, New York, Melbourne, Madrid, Cape Town, Singapore, São Paulo, Delhi

Cambridge University Press
The Edinburgh Building, Cambridge CB2 8RU, UK

www.cambridge.org
Information on this title: www.cambridge.org/9780521702058

First published 2008

Printed in the United Kingdom at the University Press, Cambridge

A catalogue record for this publication is available from the British Library

ISBN-13 978-0-521-70205-8

Contents

☕ Social and Travel

🖱 Work and Study

Appendices

Map of the book

Unit number	Title	Topic	How to ...
9	**Don't worry!**	First aid and accidents	o identify the most important parts of sentences o follow instructions in a first aid manual and give first aid o find out about treatment at Accident and Emergency (A&E)
10	**What's in the news?**	Newspapers	o use headlines to predict the content of newspaper articles o understand short newspaper articles o identify words that are useful to you
11	**I'll check my email**	Keeping in touch	o work out the main purpose of an email o understand email abbreviations and 'smileys' o identify different types of email and deal with them
12	**Is that spelt correctly?**	Checking spellings	o identify British English and American English spellings o use a dictionary to find American English spellings o add words to the computer's customized dictionary o identify incorrect spellings
13	**How do I join?**	Using a library	o put the sentences of a text into your own words o find out about a library, what you can borrow and what you have to pay for
14	**At the sports centre**	Staff noticeboard	o use a variety of approaches when reading texts o read advertisements on a noticeboard and decide what you are interested in o find out about taking up a new sport and having lessons
15	**I'd like to work here**	Working in a music store	o use a dictionary with English definitions to find out the meaning of words o find out about jobs and benefits on a company website o choose a job you are interested in
16	**Just the job!**	Finding a job	o skim a page of advertisements in a newspaper to find out which ones are most useful to you o understand job advertisements and choose a job which suits you o complete a job application form

Social and Travel (units 9–11)

Work and Study (units 12–16)

Acknowledgements

I would like to thank Nóirín Burke and Caroline Thiriau, of Cambridge University Press, for their help and guidance in the writing of this book. I am also grateful to Jane Coates and Claire Cole for their involvement in its editing, Linda Matthews for overseeing its production, and Stephanie White and Paul Fellows for its design.

My thanks also go to Ian Lees, Marcos Martos Higueras and Maria-Jose Luque Arrabal for their help in finding the texts.

The author and publishers are grateful to the following reviewers for their valuable insights and suggestions:

Steve Banfield, United Arab Emirates; Ildiko Berke, Hungary; Ian Chisholm, United Kingdom; Alper Darici, Turkey; Stephanie Dimond-Bayir, United Kingdom; Rosie Ganne, United Kingdom; Professor Peter Gray, Japan; Duncan Hindmarch, United Kingdom; Elif Isler, Turkey; Kathy Kolarik, Australia; L. Krishnaveni, Malaysia; Steve Miller, United Kingdom; Ersoy Osman, United Kingdom.

The authors and publishers acknowledge the following sources of copyright material and are grateful for the permissions granted. While every effort has been made, it has not always been possible to identify the sources of all the material used, or to trace all copyright holders. If any omissions are brought to our notice, we will be happy to include the appropriate acknowledgements on reprinting.

p. 13: the information from Oxfam and their logo from www.oxfam.org.uk and other sources is reproduced with the permission of Oxfam GB, Oxfam House, John Smith Drive, Cowley, Oxford OX4 2JY www.oxfam.org.uk. Oxfam GB does not necessarily endorse any text or activities that accompany the materials; pp. 15–16, 19: the extracts from the Royal Mail 'Airmail Made Easy' leaflet. Used with permission from Royal Mail Group Ltd; p. 19: the page from Brighton Theatre Royal programme. Copyright © Theatre Royal Brighton. Used with permission from Theatre Royal, Brighton; pp. 20–21: the pages from the Duke of York Picturehouse brochure. Copyright © City Screen Limited. Used with permission from City Screen Limited; pp. 22–23: the webpages on Airport security' from the BAA website www.baa.com/security. Copyright © BAA Limited; p. 24: 'A Customs Guide for Travellers Entering the UK' from HM Revenues and Customs. Crown Copyright © 2007; pp. 30–33: the webpages from www.hostelbookers.com. Copyright © Hostelbookers 2002–2007; pp. 34–37: the pages from the Table Mountain Cableway Brochure. Used by permission of Table Mountain Aerial Cableway Company Limited; p. 39: the 'Orange products and prices brochure'. Used by kind permission of Orange; p. 40: the BT phone box notice Copyright © British Telecommunications PLC. Used by permission of British Telecommunications PLC; p. 42: the 'Cuts and Grazes' extract from Practical First Aid. Copyright © 2003 Dorling Kindersley Limited. Text copyright © 2003 Red Cross Society; p. 44: the leaflet 'How do Accident and Emergency Departments work?' from the NHS Direct website www.nhsdirect.nhs.uk. Crown Copyright © 2007; pp. 46–47,

56: articles from arbroathblogspot.com; pp. 48, 73, 92–95: the dictionary entries from Cambridge Learner's Dictionary, 3rd Edition. Used by permission of Cambridge University Press; p. 48: the article by Geoff Maynard, Daily Express 16 September 2006; p. 56: the YHA logo and text. Reproduced by permission of YHA (England and Wales) Ltd; pp. 58–59: the extracts from the 'Tivoli Gardens' brochure from Copenhagen This Week. Used by permission of Copenhagen This Week. www.ctw.com; p. 61: the 'British and American English' text from Improve Your Spelling by George Davidson (Penguin Books, 2005). Copyright © George Davidson 2005; p. 62: the 'Correcting spelling mistakes' extract from Microsoft® Word 2000 Step by Step (9781572319707). Microsoft Press 1999. All rights reserved; p. 62: the extract from 'Using Autocorrect' from Shortcuts in Word 2000 by Sue Etherington (Dorling Kindersley, 2002). Copyright © Dorling Kindersley, 2002. Reproduced by permission of Penguin Books Ltd; Copyright © Express Newspapers; pp. 65–66: the webpage and leaflets 'Join a library' and 'Paying for library services'. Copyright © Oxfordshire County Council. Used by permission of Oxfordshire County Council; p. 70: the 'Real Tennis' advert. Used by permission of The Cambridge University Real Tennis Club; pp. 72–75: webpages from and HMV Logo www.hmvcareers.co.uk. The HMV logo is a registered® Trade Mark of HMV Group plc through HMV (IP) Limited and reproduced here by kind authorization of HMV Group plc.

The publishers are grateful to the following for permission to reproduce copyright photographs and material:

Key: l = left, c = centre, r = right, t = top, b = bottom

Alamy/©WoodyStock for p. 10(b), /©Guy Somerset for p. 10(c), /©Vario images GmbH & Co, KG for p. 10(e), /©Bramwellslocker for p. 26(a), /©D Hurst for p. 26(b), /©Peter Scholey for p. 26(c), /©David Cook/www.blueshiftstudios.co.uk for p. 26(d), /©Rodolfo Arpia for p. 26(e), /©MaRoDee Photography for p. 26(f); Corbis Images/©Tom & Dee Ann McCarthy for p. 10(a), /©Randy Faris for p. 72 (tl), /©Simon Jarratt for p. 72 (cl), /©Bill Varie for p. 72 (br); DK Images/©Andy Crawford for p. 64; HMV for p. 75; Punchstock/©Digital Vision for p. 10(d), /©Stockbyte for p. 72 (cr), /©Blend Images for p. 72 (bl), /©Blend Images for p. 72 (tr); Rex for p. 10(f); Shutterstock/©Ljupco Smokovski for p. 70; p. 41 Coins courtesy of Royal Mint; Solent News & Photo Agency for p. 48; Tivoli Gardens, Denmark for p. 58; Veronique Vial for p. 55.

Illustrations:

Kathy Baxendale pp. 22t, 42, 61; Mark Duffin pp. 12, 14, 15, 16, 27, 41, 43, 44, 57, 69, 70, 72; Kamae Design pp. 40; Valeryia Steadman pp. 68; Mark Watkinson pp. 22b, 31

Text design and page make-up: Kamae Design, Oxford
Cover design: Kamae Design, Oxford
Cover photo: © Getty
Picture research: Hilary Luckcock

Introduction
To the student

Who is *Real Reading 2* for?

You can use this book if you are a student at pre-intermediate level and you want to improve your English reading. You can use the book alone without a teacher or you can use it in a classroom with a teacher.

How will *Real Reading 2* help me with my reading?

Real Reading 2 contains texts for everyday reading practice, for example leaflets, notices, websites, newspapers, etc. It is designed to help you with reading you will need to do in English at home or when visiting another country.

The exercises in each unit help you develop useful skills such as working out the meaning of unknown words from context and ignoring parts of the text which are not useful to you. It is designed to help you with reading you will need to do in English at home or when visiting another country.

How is *Real Reading 2* organized?

The book has 16 units and is divided into two sections:
- Units 1–11 – social and travel situations
- Units 12–16 – work and study situations

Every unit is divided into Reading A and Reading B and has:
- *Get ready to read*: to introduce you to the topic of the unit
- *Learning tip*: to help you improve your learning
- *Class bonus*: an exercise you can do with other students or friends
- *Focus on*: to help you study useful grammar or vocabulary
- *Did you know?*: extra information about vocabulary, different cultures or the topic of the unit
- *Extra practice*: an extra exercise for more practice
- *Can-do checklist*: to help you think about what you learnt in the unit

After each section there is a review unit. The reviews help you practise the skills you learn in each section.

At the back of the book you can find:
- *Appendices*: contain lists of *Useful language* and *Learning tips* for every unit and information about *Using a dictionary*
- *Answer key* (only in self-study edition): gives correct answers and possible answers for exercises that have more than one answer.

How can I use *Real Reading 2*?

The units at the end of the book are more difficult than the units at the beginning of the book. However, you do not need to do the units in order. It is better to choose the units that are most interesting for you and to do them in the order you prefer.

There are many different ways you can use this book. We suggest you work in this way:
- Look in the *Contents* list and find a unit that interests you.
- Prepare yourself for reading by working through the *Get ready to read* exercises.
- Look at Appendix 1: *Useful language* for the unit.
- Do the exercises in Reading A. Use the example answers to guide you. Put the *Learning tip* into practice (either in Reading A or Reading B).
- Do the exercises in Reading B.
- Check your answers either with your teacher or with the *Answer Key*.
- If you want to do more work, do the *Extra practice* activity.
- At the end of the unit, think about what you have learnt and complete the *Can-do checklist*.
- Look at the list of *Learning tips* in *Appendix 2* and decide which other tips you have used in the unit.

Introduction
To the teacher

What is *Cambridge English Skills*?

Real Reading 2 is one of 12 books in the *Cambridge English Skills* series. The series also contains *Real Writing* and *Real Listening & Speaking* books and offers skills training to students from elementary to advanced level. All the books are available in with-answers and without-answers editions.

Level	Book	Author
Elementary CEF: A2 Cambridge ESOL: KET NQF Skills for life: Entry 2	Real Reading 1 with answers	Liz Driscoll
	Real Reading 1 without answers	Liz Driscoll
	Real Writing 1 with answers and audio CD	Graham Palmer
	Real Writing 1 without answers	Graham Palmer
	Real Listening & Speaking 1 with answers and audio CD	Miles Craven
	Real Listening & Speaking 1 without answers	Miles Craven
Pre-intermediate CEF: B1 Cambridge ESOL: PET NQF Skills for life: Entry 3	Real Reading 2 with answers	Liz Driscoll
	Real Reading 2 without answers	Liz Driscoll
	Real Writing 2 with answers and audio CD	Graham Palmer
	Real Writing 2 without answers	Graham Palmer
	Real Listening & Speaking 2 with answers and audio CD	Sally Logan & Craig Thaine
	Real Listening & Speaking 2 without answers	Sally Logan & Craig Thaine
Intermediate to upper-intermediate CEF: B2 Cambridge ESOL: FCE NQF Skills for life: Level 1	Real Reading 3 with answers	Liz Driscoll
	Real Reading 3 without answers	Liz Driscoll
	Real Writing 3 with answers and audio CD	Roger Gower
	Real Writing 3 without answers	Roger Gower
	Real Listening & Speaking 3 with answers and audio CD	Miles Craven
	Real Listening & Speaking 3 without answers	Miles Craven
Advanced CEF: C1 Cambridge ESOL: CAE NQF Skills for life: Level 2	Real Reading 4 with answers	Liz Driscoll
	Real Reading 4 without answers	Liz Driscoll
	Real Writing 4 with answers and audio CD	Simon Haines
	Real Writing 4 without answers	Simon Haines
	Real Listening & Speaking 4 with answers and audio CD	Miles Craven
	Real Listening & Speaking 4 without answers	Miles Craven

Where are the teacher's notes?

The series is accompanied by a dedicated website containing detailed teaching notes and extension ideas for every unit of every book. Please visit www.cambridge.org/englishskills to access the *Cambridge English Skills* teacher's notes.

What are the main aims of *Real Reading 2*?

- To help students develop reading skills in accordance with the ALTE (Association of Language Testers in Europe) Can-do statements. These statements describe what language users can typically do at different levels and in different contexts. Visit www.alte.org for further information.
- To encourage autonomous learning by focusing on learner training.

What are the key features of *Real Reading 2*?

- It is aimed at pre-intermediate learners of English at level B1 of the Council of Europe's CEFR (Common European Framework of Reference for Languages).
- The book contains 16 four-page units, divided into two sections: *Social and Travel* and *Work and Study*.
- *Real Reading 2* units are divided into Reading A and Reading B and contain:
  - *Get ready to read* warm-up exercises to get students thinking about the topic
  - *Learning tip*s which give students advice on how to improve their reading and their learning
  - *Class bonus* communication activities for pairwork and group work so that you can adapt the material to suit your classes
  - *Focus on* exercises which provide contextualized practice in particular grammar or vocabulary areas
  - *Did you know?* boxes which provide notes on cultural or linguistic differences between English-speaking countries, or factual information on the topic of the unit
  - *Extra practice* extension tasks which provide more real world reading practice
  - *Can-do checklists* at the end of every unit to encourage students to think about what they have learnt
- There are two review units to practise skills that have been introduced in the units.
- It has an international feel and contains a range of texts from English-speaking – and other – countries.
- It can be used as self-study material, in class, or as supplementary homework material.

What is the best way to use *Real Reading 2* in the classroom?

The book is designed so that the units may be used in any order, although the more difficult units naturally appear near the end of the book, in the *Work and Study* section.

You can consult the unit-by-unit teacher's notes at www.cambridge.org/englishskills for detailed teaching ideas. However, broadly speaking, different parts of the book can be approached in the following ways:

- *Useful language*: You can use the *Useful language* lists in *Appendix 1* to preteach or revise the vocabulary from the unit you are working on.
- *Get ready to read*: It is a good idea to use this section as an introduction to the topic. Students can work on the exercises in pairs or groups. Many of these require students to answer questions about their personal experience. These questions can be used as prompts for discussion. Some exercises contain a problem-solving element that students can work on together. Other exercises aim to clarify key vocabulary in the unit. You can present these vocabulary items directly to students.
- *Learning tips*: You can ask students to read and discuss these in an open-class situation. An alternative approach is for you to create a series of discussion questions associated with the *Learning tip*. Students can discuss their ideas in pairs or small groups followed by open-class feedback. The *Learning tip* acts as a reflective learning tool to help promote learner autonomy.
- *Class bonuses*: The material in these activities aims to provide freer practice. You can set these up carefully, then take the role of observer during the activity so that students carry out the task freely. You can make yourself available to help students or analyze the language they produce during the activity.
- *Extra practice*: These activities can be set as homework or out-of-class projects for your students. Alternatively, students can do some activities in pairs during class time.
- *Can-do checklists*: Refer to these at the beginning of a lesson to explain to students what the lesson will cover and again at the end so that students can evaluate their learning for themselves.
- *Appendices*: You may find it useful to refer your students to the *Useful language*, *Learning tips* and *Using a dictionary* sections. Students can use these as general checklists to help them with their reading.

Unit 1
Is there a bank?

go to Useful language p. 82

Get ready to read

- Look at the photographs. What are these shops and services? Choose from the words in the box.

baker's	bank	butcher's
delicatessen	~~dry cleaner's~~	hairdresser's
newsagent's	optician's	stationer's
chemist's	library	travel agent's

a dry cleaner's   d library

b bakers   e optician

c   f delicatessen

- Look at the list of places again. Which places are shops? Which provide other services for customers? Write two lists.

shops	services
baker's	bank

- Add some other places to the two lists above.

- Imagine you are doing a language course in Britain. Look at your list of shops and services. Which shops and services are most important to you? (✗ = not very important, ✓ = important, ✓✓ = very important)

A Welcome to Summertown

1 Imagine you are doing a language course in Summertown and you see the leaflet on the opposite page on the school noticeboard. Look quickly at the leaflet. What is it about? Tick ✓ one of the boxes.

a shops in Summertown ☐
b services in Summertown ☐
c shops and services in Summertown ☒

Learning tip

We sometimes look through a text to find a particular piece of information. This type of reading is called *scanning*. When we scan, we don't read every word. We find the information we're looking for and then stop reading. We don't pay any attention to the rest of the text.

2 Scan the leaflet on the opposite page and find the answers to these questions. Answer *yes* or *no*.

a Is there a bike rental store in Summertown?   yes
b Is there a post office?
c Is there an internet café?
d Is there a cinema?
e Is there a dry cleaner's?
f Is there an optician's?

Welcome to
Summertown!

We hope you will enjoy your stay here! Summertown is a busy community which has built up around Banbury Road, the main road heading north from the centre of Oxford. It is a mainly residential area. Here are some notes which we hope will help make your stay enjoyable.

Oxford City Centre is within easy reach. Several buses – 2, 7, 17, 25, 27, 59 and 218 – run frequently to and from the centre. Alternatively, you can rent or buy a bike and cycle down Banbury Road in about ten minutes. (You can hire a bike at Summertown Cycles, or buy your own.)

Shops and other services

You don't need to go into Oxford for your shopping as you will find everything you need here in Summertown. Most shops are in Banbury Road. There are three supermarkets for food shopping. The Co-op (at the southern end of the shoping area) is open until 10pm on weekday evenings and has the longest opening hours. Other specialist food shops include a fruit shop, a delicatessen, a Lebanese shop and takeaway, a butcher's shop and two baker's. Unless otherwise stated, shopping hours are from 9.30am until 5.30pm, Monday–Saturday.

There used to be three newsagent's in Summertown, but now there is only one. Martins is at the northern end of the shopping area. Martins can order foreign newspapers for you. Speak to one of the sales assistants if you'd like to arrange this. You can also buy stamps here. There is no longer a post office in Summertown. The nearest post office is in the centre of Oxford.

There are three banks in Summertown – Lloyds, HSBC and Barclays. Opening hours are 9.00am–4.30pm. All of them have ATM machines outside.

Other shops in Banbury Road include a stationer's, a book store, a health shop and a card shop. There is also an internet café, a computer shop and a branch of MAIL BOXES ETC. which will ship your possessions home for you at the end of your stay.

Summertown Library is in South Parade, which is at the northern end of Banbury Road. The library is open every day except Wednesday and everyone is welcome. You'll find lots of information about the area here, and you can also read the newspapers.

There isn't a cinema in Summertown, but there are two video rental stores. Blockbuster, in Banbury Road, offers the usual mainstream films. Videosyncratic, in South Parade, on the other hand, has a wide selection of foreign films.

Summertown's travel agent's and launderette are both in South Parade. There is also a dry cleaner's in Banbury Road. You can get your photos developed there too. For your medical needs, there are two chemist's in Banbury Road. There is also an optician's.

There are several hairdresser's, both for men and women, in Summertown. Two of them – Wendy Burnett's and Anthony Lawrence – also offer a range of beauty treatments.

3 Which of the services in Exercise 2 are in Banbury Road? Which are in South Parade? Write *BR* or *SP* after your *yes* answers in Exercise 2.

4 What other shops and services are there in Summertown? Write a list.

----

5 Are these sentences true (T) or false (F)?
  a There is a good bus service into Oxford from Summertown. ..T..
  b Most shops in Summertown are closed on Sundays. T....
  c The Co-op supermarket is opposite the newsagent's. F..
  d The newsagent's sells stamps. ......
  e The best day to go to the library is Wednesday. F...
  f There are two hairdresser's in Summertown. T......

Class bonus

Write some questions about the text like those in Exercise 2 or some true/false statements like those in Exercise 5. Give your questions/statements to another student. Answer your partner's questions or decide if his/her statements are true or false.

6 Are there any other shops or services you would like to find in Summertown?

E✗tra practice

Imagine you are doing a language course in another British town or city. Look at the website for this town/city. Scan the website to find out if it has all the services you noted in *Get ready to read*.

B I saw it in the window

1 Complete these sentences.

a
> If I needed some money,
> I'd go to a _____bank_____ .

b
> If I needed to wash my clothes,
> I'd go to a dry·cleaner's

c
> If I wanted to send some emails,
> I'd go to a/an internet café

d
> If I needed to send a parcel,
> I'd go to a _____ .

e
> If I needed my eyes tested,
> I'd go to an opticians's

f
> If I wanted to rent a bike,
> I'd go to a biker's
> _____ .

2 Look at these notices from windows of shops and places in Summertown which provide other services. Where would you see each notice?

a ____video rental store____
b _____
c _____
d _____
e _____
f _____
g _____
h _____

---

a

RENTAL MADNESS
2 for £7 for 2 nights
or
3 for £9 for 2 nights
MIX & MATCH
on all movies & games
including new releases

b

Discover

Fresh fruit and veg
Bread fresh from the oven
Fresh fish and meat
Hot food to go
and much more . . .

c

INTERNET from 90p an hour
3p per minute (£1 minimum) PAY AS YOU GO
£5 budget card   5 hours
(unlimited logins last 90 days)
£10 budget card   11 hours + 7 minutes
(unlimited logins last 90 days)
"Best value in Oxford"

d

Revised prices from April

restyling	£19.50
wash / cut / blow dry	£18.50
wet cut / blow dry	£17.50
children's wet cut / blow dry	£10.50
OAPs from	£9.00
Beard trim	£3.50

These prices include all extras, i.e. gel, conditioner, hairspray, etc.
Prices may vary due to length of hair and time taken on certain styles.
Please note: Discounts for students Monday only.

e

Repeat prescription collection & delivery
Disposal of medicines
Holiday and travel health advice
Development & printing
Medical advice
Treatment for minor ailments

f

Sorry, our systems need a maintenance check, which means customers won't be able to withdraw cash from any of our ATMs using Barclay, LINK or VISA cards for a few hours on Sunday morning.

**Sunday 3rd September
from 1am to 6am**

g

IDEAL EYES Ltd

We are a local independent company and are proud to announce we will soon be opening our third practice.

We take pride in offering a friendly, professional service to all our patients, private or NHS.

For further information, contact 01865 244699.

h

*OPEN 7.00am
LAST WASH 7.00pm
CLOSE 8.30PM*

*SERVICE WASH
9.30am – 2.30pm
Monday – Friday*

In order to assist customers, members of staff – on a voluntary basis – are willing to complete washing which will be collected later. This is a private arrangement between customer and staff, and we do not accept responsibility for any loss or damage to the said washing.

3 Scan the notices and answer these questions. The question letters match the notice letters.

a What exactly can you rent for £9?
3 movies or games for 2 nights

b Can you get takeaway meals here?

c How much time do you get for the cheaper budget card?

d Why might some prices be higher?

e Do they only deal with medicine and health?

f When can't you use the ATM machine?

g Whose phone number is given?

h What is the latest time you can start your washing?

Focus on ...
for and from

We use *for*
– to show an amount of money and time: *2 for £7 for 2 nights*
– when something can be used by someone or something:
Discounts for students Monday only

We use *from* to show
– where something started: *Bread fresh from the oven*
– when something started: *Revised prices from April 2006*
– the starting price: *INTERNET from 90p an hour*

Complete these sentences with *for* or *from*.
a The launderette is open ___from___ 7.00am.
b Fresh fish comes _____ the sea.
c You can buy the cheapest budget card _____ £5.
d The launderette is _____ people without washing machines.
e You can go to the supermarket _____ fresh fruit.
f A haircut costs _____ £9.

Complete these two expressions from the text.
g _____ further information, contact 01865 244699.
h We do not accept responsibility _____ any loss or damage.

4 Look at this notice from another shop in Summertown. This shop sells things, but what is different about it? Complete this sentence.

Oxfam sells things

⊗ Oxfam

Opening Times

Monday	9.30am – 5.30pm
Tuesday	9.30am – 5.30pm
Wednesday	9.30am – 5.30pm
Thursday	9.30am – 5.30pm
Friday	9.30am – 5.30pm
Saturday	9.30am – 5.30pm
Sunday	CLOSED

We are very grateful for your donated goods. Please help us by leaving them when the shop is OPEN.

Leaving donations outside the shop at any other time presents a fire risk, and donations get STOLEN.

Thank you for your co-operation.

Did you know ...?

Oxfam was started in 1942 and is the UK's largest aid agency. 'Oxfam' is short for 'Oxford Committee for Famine Relief'. Its headquarters used to be in Summertown and its first shop is in the centre of Oxford. The Summertown shop is one of 500 in the UK.

5 Look at all the notices again. Which of the shops and services would you use if you lived in Summertown?

Can-do checklist

Tick what you can do.

	Can do	Need more practice
I can scan a text to find particular pieces of information.		
I can find out about services in the area where I am staying.		
I can read notices in shop windows and find out exactly what services are available.		

Airmail, please!

go to Useful language p. 82

Get ready to read

a

> TALYA MINE
> YÜKSEL CD NO 9
> DAIRE 10
> KIZILAY-ANKARA

b

London

c

> Żrinka kolento
> Raba Wy_na 500
> 34-721 Poland

> Mr Taro Tanaka
> 5-2-1 Ginza
> Chuo-Ku
> Tokyo 170-3293

d

- Look at the items. Circle the correct word.
  - a letter / *packet* / postcard / package
  - b letter / packet / postcard / package
  - c letter / packet / postcard / package
  - d letter / packet / postcard / package

- Which of the items do you usually receive in these situations?
  - a You've bought a CD-ROM on the Internet.   _packet_
  - b You've opened a new bank account.   ....
  - c It's your birthday and you're expecting a large present.   ....
  - d Your best friend has gone on holiday.   ....
  - e You've phoned a hotel because you left a T-shirt there.   ....
  - f The dentist wants to change your appointment.   ....

- Which of these items might come from abroad?

- Do you ever receive letters, postcards, packets or packages from abroad?

A Can I have a sticker?

Learning tip

We often look at a text quickly to find out what it is about or to get a general idea of its meaning. We look at pictures and headings, as well as the text itself. This type of reading is called *skimming*. When we skim, we don't read every word. We get the main idea and don't pay attention to the small details.

1 You are going to read a text from a leaflet called *Mail made easy*. Skim the text on the opposite page. What is it about? Tick ✓ one of the boxes.

a sending letters and postcards within the UK ☐
b sending letters and postcards within Europe ☐
c sending letters and postcards all over the world ☐

2 Skim the text again. Which of these sentences is true? Tick ✓ one of the boxes.

a Airmail is faster but more expensive than surface mail. ☐
b Surface mail is slower and more expensive than airmail. ☐
c Airmail is cheaper and faster than surface mail. ☐

3 How do you address the envelopes? Complete the sentences.

a If you are using airmail, you ....
....
b If you are using surface mail, you ....
....

Focus on ...
pounds and pence

ab**C**def

Look at the list of airmail prices on the leaflet. Circle the figures for these prices.
a one pound forty-one (pence)
b three pounds ten (pence)
c sixty-four pence
d four pounds and two pence

Now write these prices in words. Practise saying the prices aloud.
e £0.72   _seventy-two pence_
f £1.02   ....
g £1.79   ....
h £2.14   ....
i £2.70   ....
j £3.08   ....

Sending mail abroad

What are you sending?

Letters and postcards

Letters and postcards to Europe can only be sent by Airmail – up to a maximum weight of 2kg.

Airmail

Our standard Airmail service for sending international mail to anywhere in the world quickly and cost effectively.

How to use

Stick our branded Airmail sticker – available free from Post Office® branches – on your item of mail and post it in any post box or Post Office® branch. Alternatively, you can simply write 'BY AIRMAIL – PAR AVION' in the front top left corner.

Sra Ana Jirnez
Director
Internacional SL
Mimbreras
03201 ELCH (Alicante)
SPAIN

The name of the country in CAPITALS must come last.

Our Airmail delivery aims are:

Western Europe
3 days following day of posting
Eastern Europe
4 days following day of posting
Outside Europe
5 days following day of posting

Airmail prices

Weight up to	Letters		
	Europe	World Zone 1	World Zone 2
Postcards	£0.44	£0.50	£0.50
10g	£0.44	£0.50	£0.50
20g	£0.44	£0.72	£0.72
40g	£0.64	£1.12	£1.19
60g	£0.83	£1.51	£1.66
80g	£1.02	£1.91	£2.14
100g	£1.21	£2.31	£2.61
120g	£1.41	£2.70	£3.08
140g	£1.60	£3.10	£3.55
160g	£1.79	£3.49	£4.02

Surface mail

Our economical service for sending non-urgent international mail.

How to use

Surface items should be addressed as normal.

Sra Ana Jirnez
Director
Internacional SL
Mimbreras
03201 ELCH (Alicante)
SPAIN

The name of the country in CAPITALS must come last.

Our Surface mail delivery aims are:

Western Europe
2 weeks following day of posting
Eastern Europe
4 weeks following day of posting
Outside Europe
8 to 12 weeks following day of posting

Surface mail prices

Weight up to	Letters (only to outside Europe)
Postcards	£0.42
20g	£0.42
60g	£0.72
100g	£1.02
150g	£1.43

Where is it going?

World Zone 1
World Zone 1 covers all countries not in either Europe or World Zone 2.

World Zone 2		
Australia	Korea	Philippines
China	New Zealand	Taiwan
Japan		

---

4 How much would it cost to send the following letters and postcards by airmail? Write the answers in numbers.

   a a postcard to Italy   <u>£0.44</u>

   b a letter weighing 85 grams to Australia

   c a letter to Argentina weighing 55 grams

   d a postcard to Taiwan

   e a letter to the US weighing 130 grams

   f a letter to the Czech Republic weighing 55 grams

5 Which of the postcards and letters in Exercise 4 can you send by surface mail? How much longer would they take to reach their destinations?

Class bonus

Choose some more weights and destinations for mail you want to send. Give your list to another student. Can you work out the prices for your partner?

B Can you fill this in?

1 Imagine you are in Great Britain. You are going to send the following gifts to friends and family abroad. Match the gifts with the three headings under *What are you sending?* Write the numbers in the boxes.

a   a book about British customs to your penfriend in Germany ☐

b   money to your cousin in the US who is coming to Britain next month ☐

c   a T-shirt to your brother in Australia ☐

Sending mail abroad

What are you sending?

¹ **Small packets**

This service offers you a cheaper rate if you're sending gifts, goods or commercial samples. Please write 'SMALL PACKET' in the top left corner. You can also include a letter relating to the contents. Where necessary, you should also attach a customs document. The maximum weight is 2kg.

² **Printed papers**

You can also get a cheaper rate when sending books, magazines, newspapers, leaflets and pamphlets abroad. You can include a letter relating to the contents. Please write 'PRINTED PAPERS' in the top left corner. The maximum weight to most places is 2kg or 5kg for books, leaflets and pamphlets.

³ **Valuable items**

If you're sending valuable items abroad (such as money, jewellery and precious metals), you should use the Letters or Small Packets service in conjunction with either Airsure® or International Signed For®.

Did you know ...?

Addresses in the US always include a *zip code* – a group of letters and/or numbers which are at the end. The UK equivalent is the *postcode*. Compare these two addresses. Notice that the house number is before the name of the street in both countries.

Stefano Musetti
1819 Murdoch St
Pittsburgh
PA 15217
USA
(PA stands for Pennsylvania.)

Anna Linda Torelli
Flat 1, 7 Milton St
Edinburgh
EH8 8E2
UK
(EH stands for Edinburgh.)

2 Read the section *Customs information* below. Which of the gifts in Exercise 1 do you need to send a customs declaration form with?

Customs information

You **DON'T** need to complete a customs declaration form if you're sending:

- letters, postcards and documents alone
- small packets and packages containing goods to countries in the European Union (EU).

You **DO** need to complete a customs declaration form if you're sending:

- small packets and packages containing goods to countries not in the European Union (EU).

CUSTOMS DECLARATION DÉCLARATION EN DOUANE		CN 22 May be opened officially Peut être ouvert d'office
Great Britain\Grande-Bretagne	Important!	See instructions on the back
	Gift\Cadeau	Commercial sample\Echantillon commercial
	Documents	Other\Autre *Tick one or more boxes*
Quantity and detailed description of contents (1) Quantité et description détaillée du contenu	Weight (*in kg*)(2) Poids	Value (3) Valeur
– – – – –	– – – –	– – – –
– – – – –	– – – –	– – – –

3 What do you need to write on the envelopes for items a and b? _____
_____

4 What else do you need to find out before you can post these gifts? Complete the sentences.

a   Before you post the book, you need to find out how much _____ .

b   Before you post the money, you need to find out about
_____ .

5 Read the instructions for the customs declaration form and complete the form for item c (The T-shirt weighs approximately 250g). You can ignore the French words on the form.

Instructions

[1] Give a detailed description, quantity and unit of measurement for each article, e.g. three DVDs.

[2], [3], [6] and [7] Give the weight and value of each article and the total weight and value of the item. Indicate the currency used, i.e. GBP for pounds sterling.

[8] Your signature and the date confirm your liability for the item.

CUSTOMS DECLARATION
DÉCLARATION EN DOUANE

CN 22
May be opened officially
Peut être ouvert d'office

Great Britain\Grande-Bretagne **Important!** See instructions on the back

| | Gift\Cadeau | | Commercial sample\Echantillon commercial |
| | Documents | | Other\Autre *Tick one or more boxes* |

Quantity and detailed description of contents (1) Quantité et description détaillée du contenu	Weight (*in kg*)(2) Poids	Value (3) Valeur
– – – – – – – – – – – – –	– – – –	– – –
– – – – – – – – – – – – –	– – – –	– – –
– – – – – – – – – – – – –	– – – –	– – –

For commercial items only If known, HS tariff number (4) and country of origin of goods (5) N°tarifaire du SH et pays d'origine des marchandises (si connus)	Total Weight Poids total (*in kg*) (6)	Total Value (7) Valeur totale

I, the undersigned, whose name and address are given on the item, certify that the particulars given in this declaration are correct and that this item does not contain any dangerous article or articles prohibited by legislation or by postal or customs regulations

Date and sender's signature (8)

---

6 Which parts of the form did you not need to complete?

E✗tra practice

Look at the website www.royalmail.com and find out about the Airsure® and International Signed For® (Airmail) services. Complete these sentences.
a _____ is cheaper.
b _____ does not need a signature on delivery.
c You can use _____ to any country in the world.
d The maximum weight for _____ is 2kg.

Can-do checklist

Tick what you can do.

	Can do	Need more practice
I can read a post office leaflet quickly to get a general idea of what it is about.		
I can find the information I need to decide which is the best way to send letters and postcards abroad.		
I can find out how to send packets and packages abroad.		

Unit 3
What's on?

Get ready to read

○ Which of these sentences is true for you?
Tick ✓ one box.
I never go to the theatre. ☐
I hardly ever go to the theatre. ☐
I go to the theatre about once a month. ☐
I go to the theatre two or three times a year. ☐

○ How often do you go to the cinema? Write a sentence.

○ Which of these types of show would you prefer to see
at the theatre? Put them in order. (1 = your favourite,
7 = your least favourite)
a ballet ☐   an opera ☐
a comedy ☐   a play ☐
a concert ☐   a musical ☐
a dance show ☐

go to Useful language p. 83

A At Brighton Theatre Royal

Learning tip

When you read, it isn't necessary to
understand every word in the text. You
only need to understand the parts of the
text which contain the information you are
looking for.

1 Merve is living in Brighton. Her sister
is coming to visit her in February
and Merve would like to take her
to the theatre. She is looking at the
programme for the Theatre Royal. Scan
the programme on the opposite page.
Are all the shows on in February?

2 What kind of shows are on at the
theatre? Write three sentences.

Tap Dogs is a _____
_____
_____

Did you know …?

The word *tap* has many meanings. Here
it describes a type of dancing where the
dancer wears special shoes with
pieces of metal on the bottom
which make a noise.

3 Merve's friend Kristen has seen these shows. She is
telling Merve about them. Which show does each
sentence describe? (The shows are described more
than once.)

a It was written by
Willy Russell.

b It's a show with Irish
music and dance.

Blood Brothers
_____   _____

c It has six dancers.

d It takes place in Liverpool.

_____   _____

e It has been on tour to
fifteen countries.

f It is directed by Nigel Triffitt.

_____   _____

4 What other things could Kristen say about the shows?
Write one or two more sentences about each show.
Use the sentences in Exercise 3 as models.

Blood Brothers has won four awards for Best Musical in London.
_____
_____
_____

DEIN PERRY'S TAP DOGS

DIRECTED AND DESIGNED BY NIGEL TRIFFITT

A smash hit since its first performance in 1995, Olivier Award-winning *Tap Dogs* returns to Brighton as part of an international tour. Dressed in Levis and Blundstone Boots, the explosive cast of six strapping Aussie tap dancers return to the Theatre Royal stage in a feast of stylish routines.

The raw energy of *Tap Dogs* has thrilled and astonished audiences across the globe in equal measure. They were the toast of the Sydney Olympics, entertaining over 3 billion people at the opening ceremony.

You won't want to miss this – the hottest show on legs!

Mon 7 – Sat 12 Feb

Did you hear the story of the Johnstone twins?

Set in Willy Russell's native Liverpool, *Blood Brothers* tells the tale of twin boys, separated at birth only to be re-united by a twist of fate and a mother's guilty secret.

Scooping up no less than four awards for Best Musical in London, seven Tony nominations on Broadway, and receiving a standing ovation at every performance, *Blood Brothers* is truly unforgettable.

Mon 21 – Sat 26 Feb

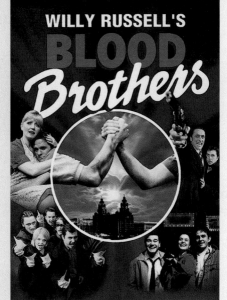

WILLY RUSSELL'S BLOOD Brothers

SPIRIT of the DANCE

With special guests

Ireland's Three Tenors

Irish in origin, this powerful show combines Irish Dance with the sensual Latino rhythms of Flamenco and Red Hot Salsa in a thrilling production of strength and passion.

Spirit of the Dance is one of the most successful shows to come out of Ireland and has been seen by more than thirty million people in fifteen countries around the world.

Special guests in this year's show are Ireland's Three Tenors, who bring a selection of songs and some of the greatest voices ever heard to *Spirit of the Dance*.

Not one Irish dance shoe steps out of line as their thunderous feet perform as one, with an excitement that leaves the audience screaming for more.

Mon 28 Feb – Sat 5 March

Class bonus

Work with a partner. Read out your sentences from Exercise 4, but begin the sentences with *It* – for example: *It has won four awards for Best Musical in London.* Work out which show your partner is describing.

5 Merve's sister likes dancing. Which show do you think Merve will buy tickets for? Why?

6 Would you like to go to any of these shows? Which one(s) would you choose? Why?

Focus on ...
vocabulary

There are lots of useful words in this section about going to the theatre. Read the definitions of some of the words. Write each word.

a acting, singing, dancing, playing music to entertain people
   p e r f o r m a n c e

b a prize given to someone/something for their achievement
   a _ _ _ _

c all the actors/performers in a play/show c _ _ _

d the raised area in a theatre where actors perform s _ _ _ _

e when people stand when clapping to show that they have enjoyed something very much
   s _ _ _ _ _ _ _ _ o _ _ _ _ _ _

f the people who sit and watch a performance at a theatre
   a _ _ _ _ _ _ _

B The Duke of York's Picturehouse

1 Merve's friend Kristen asks her if she would like to go and see *The History Boys* on Friday. Answer these questions.

  a Have you heard of the film?

  b Have you seen it?

  c Do you know anything about it?

2 Skim what Kristen says about *The History Boys*. Would you like to see the film?

> It's about eight boys who are studying history at school. They all want to go to Oxford or Cambridge University. They have three teachers – an old English teacher, a new young teacher who has recently left university, and the only woman teacher on the staff – who try and help them to get a university place. The film is funny most of the time, but a little bit sad as well. I've heard it's very enjoyable and not too difficult to understand.

3 Merve and Kristen decide to go and see the film at 4.30pm. Kristen is a member of the Picturehouse, but Merve is not. Scan the page from the cinema brochure below. How much will each of their tickets cost?

4 Merve then remembers that she is going to the dentist's at 4.00pm on Friday. Scan the text and complete these sentences.

  a Their tickets will cost a total of .... if they go to the later show.

  b Their tickets would cost a total of .... if Merve had a student card.

Did you know ...?

If you are a student, you can get *concessions* – reductions in the price of tickets for the cinema/theatre, buses/trains, etc. You will need a valid student card with a photo in order to prove that you are a student.

Cinema information

Ticket prices:

DAYTIME
(Films commencing before 5pm)

Full price. £5.50

Members. £4.00

Concessions £4.50

EVENINGS & WEEKEND
(Films commencing at or after 5pm weekdays, all day at weekends and on Bank Holidays)

Full price. £6.50

Members. £5.00

Concessions £5.50

MEMBERSHIP

Single £25.00

Joint £40.00

Concessions £18.00

PROGRAMME MAILING LIST

For one year £10.00

PLEASE NOTE

Advance web/phone booking fee £1.50 (waived for members).

How to pay:

- The Box Office opens 30 minutes before the first performance and closes 15 minutes after the start of the last performance.
- VISA, Masterclass, Solo, Electron, Switch and Maestro cards accepted. Solo and Electron are only accepted in person.
- Please have your card to hand when you telephone.

Advance booking:

- FROM THE BOX OFFICE: During usual opening hours.
- BY TELEPHONE: 08708 505 465. Please have your card to hand. Bookings can be made several weeks in advance, but no later than 15 minutes before the performance. There is a £1.50 booking fee (waived for members). Please bring your card to the cinema. Electron & Solo not accepted over the phone.
- ONLINE BOOKING: www.picturehouses.co.uk
  Customers receive immediate confirmation if seats are available. Bookings can be made up to 15 minutes before the screening. Please bring your card with you. Please note advance web booking fee £1.50 (waived for members).
- PLEASE NOTE: Latecomers are admitted at the manager's discretion and not after 15 minutes from the film starting.
  Right of admission is reserved by the management.

Getting to the Duke of York's

BUS: 5/5A/5B frequent from town centre; night buses to Falmer. TRAIN: Brighton station 15 mins; London Road station 5 mins (evenings: every 30 mins to Falmer until 11.35). PARKING: multi-storey off London Rd (free after 6pm). Please avoid parking in surrounding streets as it can cause a nuisance for residents.

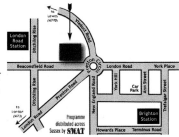

5 Friday evening is a popular time to go to the cinema, so the girls decide to book their tickets in advance. Scan the text on the opposite page and complete the chart.

	How can they book their tickets?	Can they pay cash or do they need a credit card?	Is there an extra charge for booking in this way?
a	They can go to the box office.	They can pay cash or by credit card.	No
b	They can		
c	They		

6 Merve thinks she might become a member of the Picturehouse. Kristen is explaining what you get when you join. Look at another section of the brochure on the right and decide if what Kristen says is true (T) or false (F).

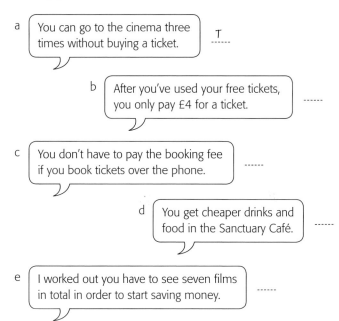

a You can go to the cinema three times without buying a ticket. ——T——

b After you've used your free tickets, you only pay £4 for a ticket. ——————

c You don't have to pay the booking fee if you book tickets over the phone. ——————

d You get cheaper drinks and food in the Sanctuary Café. ——————

e I worked out you have to see seven films in total in order to start saving money. ——————

Become a member of the Duke of York's Picturehouse

NOW YOU CAN WATCH EVEN MORE FILMS FOR LESS MONEY WITH OUR BIGGER, BETTER MEMBERSHIP OFFER:

- 3 free tickets per person (worth up to £19.50)
- £1.50 discount on all your tickets, with no booking fees to pay
- £25 single membership, £40 joint membership, £18 concessions
- FREE preview screenings
- the best of everything the Duke of York's has to offer, including priority booking for special events and discounts on the balcony box
- plus our brochure mailed to you, email listings, discounts around town and at all other Picturehouse cinemas
- 10% discount at the Sanctuary Café

7 Would you want to become a member of a cinema if you were living in Britain? Why? / Why not?

E✗tra practice

Find out where you can see English-language films in your town or city. Go and see a film. Alternatively, rent a DVD. This will probably have subtitles in your own language, which will make the film easier to understand.

Can-do checklist

Tick what you can do.

	Can do	Need more practice
I can understand a text without knowing the meaning of every word.		
I can read a theatre programme and choose a show I would like to see.		
I can read a cinema brochure, and find out about paying for tickets and membership.		

Unit4
What's in your luggage?

go to Useful language p. 83

Get ready to read

- Match the words with the pictures. Write the letters in the boxes.
  bumbag [d] hairdryer [ ] handbag [ ] laptop [ ]
  penknife [ ] rucksack [ ] suitcase [ ] walking stick [ ]

- Which of these items do you take on holiday with you?

- Imagine you are flying abroad on holiday. Where do you do these things? Tick ✓ the correct place in the chart.

	Departure airport	Arrival airport
a check in your luggage	✓	
b show your passport		
c show your boarding card		
d go through Security		
e collect your checked-in luggage		
f go through Customs		

A Airport security

1 You are going to fly from Manchester to Athens for the weekend. The day before you fly, you hear on the news that security has been increased at all British airports. You decide to look on the Internet, and this is what you find. Skim the webpage. What is it about? Tick ✓ one of the boxes.

a checked-in luggage [ ]
b hand luggage [ ]
c checked-in luggage and hand luggage [ ]

Did you know …?

The words *luggage* and *baggage* are synonyms (they have the same meaning). However, passengers usually talk about their *luggage* and airlines usually talk about *baggage*.

http://www.baa.com/security

ⓘ Airport security measures

The following items are prohibited in hand luggage. If you have any of these things, you must put them in your checked-in baggage (suitcases, etc.) or dispose of them safely. You cannot take these items through Security.

Any items purchased after Security can be taken on board. Special restrictions may apply to items taken onto flights to the US.

✓ One bag only
35cm
45cm
16cm
Maximum dimensions

✗ No liquids
No cosmetics
No toiletries
No gels or pastes including foodstuffs
No sharp items
No lighters
Not allowed through Security or in luggage. Please throw them away safely.

Learning tip

As you read, try to work out the meaning of unknown words. Use pictures where possible. Find other words in the text which can help you. For example, find a synonym (a word with a similar meaning to the unknown word), an antonym (a word which means the opposite), or an example. Only use a dictionary to check your guesses.

2 You had planned to take the following things with you to Greece. Why can't you take them through Security? Complete the chart with the singular form of words in the webpage on the opposite page.

	You can't take	because it's
a	some skin cream	a toiletry
b	a penknife	
c	some hair gel	

3 You had also planned to take the following things in your hand luggage. Can you take them through Security? (✓ = yes, ✗ = no) Leave the box empty if the answer is not clear from the notice.

a a bottle of water for the journey ✗
b a toothbrush and some toothpaste ☐
c a laptop ☐
d a cigarette lighter ☐

4 Here are five words/expressions from the webpage on the opposite page. Read the webpage carefully and <u>underline</u> them. Find five other words/expressions which have similar meanings (synonyms) and write them down. (The words in the list come before the words with a similar meaning.)

a measures ..... restrictions .....
b items .....
c prohibited .....
d luggage .....
e dispose of them .....

5 Scan the second part of the webpage *Further passenger information* on the right. Can you take your laptop through Security?

6 Read the second part of the webpage again. If you buy the other items in Exercise 3 (a, b, and d) in the departure lounge, can you take them onto the plane?

Further passenger information

1 **Please note:** Other small bags, such as handbags, may be carried within the single item of cabin baggage. All items carried by passengers will be x-ray screened.

2 All laptops and large electrical items (e.g. hairdryer) must be removed from the bag and placed in a tray so that such items neither obscure nor are obscured by the bag.

3 Pushchairs and walking aids are permitted but must be x-ray screened. Wheelchairs are allowed but they must be searched thoroughly.

4 **Before Security:** All shops and catering outlets are open to all passengers, but any liquids and gels purchased must be packed into your luggage for check-in. Any other purchases must fit into your hand luggage.

5 **Once through Security**: All shops and catering outlets are open to all passengers. If you are travelling to any destination except the USA then you can take all items purchased in the departure lounge into the aircraft cabin.

6 **If you are travelling to the USA:** Extra restrictions are in place. No toiletries or cosmetics purchased in the departure lounge will be allowed into the aircraft cabin and any drinks or liquid items must be consumed before boarding. Food, however, is allowed. Passengers boarding flights to the USA and items they are carrying, including those acquired after the central screening point, will be subjected to secondary search at the gate and any liquids discovered will be removed.

7 <u>Underline</u> these five words/expressions in the second part of the webpage. Find other words/expressions in the first part of the webpage on the opposite page which have related meanings. Are the words synonyms (S) or antonyms (A)? More than one answer is sometimes possible.

a single item of
  cabin baggage ..... one bag only ..... S
b permitted ..... ☐
c except ..... ☐
d are in place ..... ☐
e acquired ..... ☐

8 A friend of yours is travelling to the US. Can your friend buy a bottle of water, and a toothbrush and toothpaste in the departure lounge and take them onto the plane?

B Anything to declare?

1 Look at the countries in the box. Divide them into two groups – European and non-European. Write two lists.

~~Austria~~	Brazil	Canada
Greece	Japan	Poland
Saudi Arabia		Sweden
the Netherlands		Tunisia

European	Non-European
Austria	....
....	....
....	....
....	....
....	....

Class bonus

Work in pairs. How many countries can you name in five minutes? Write two lists. The winning pair is the pair with the most countries.

2 Skim this customs guide for travellers entering the UK. Complete the sentences with the numbers 1–6.

a Parts ...., ... and .... are about what you can bring in.

b Parts ...., ... and .... are about how you should go through Customs.

Did you know …?

The European Union is an economic and political alliance between European countries which was set up in 1958. The six original members were Belgium, France, West Germany, Italy, Luxembourg and the Netherlands. They were joined by the UK, Denmark and the Republic of Ireland in 1973. There are now 27 members.

1

TRAVELLING TO THE UK FROM THE EUROPEAN UNION (EU)

If you have already paid tax on goods in an EU country, you don't have to pay any tax – or duty – on them when you bring them into the UK. However, if you bring in alcohol or tobacco, this must be for your own use (you mustn't sell these goods). A customs officer may ask you questions about alcohol or tobacco goods which he/she suspects are for a commercial purpose.

2 TRAVELLING TO THE UK FROM OUTSIDE THE EUROPEAN UNION (EU)

When travelling from a non-European country, you can bring the following duty-free goods into the UK for your own use. This means that you don't pay UK tax on them.

200 cigarettes OR
100 cigarillos OR
50 cigars OR
250g of tobacco

2 LITRES of still table wine

1 LITRE of spirits or strong liqueurs over 22% volume OR
2 LITRES of fortified wine, sparkling wine or other liqueurs

60cc of perfume

250cc of eau de toilette

£145 worth of all other goods including gifts and souvenirs

3 IF YOU HAVE ANY MORE THAN THESE ALLOWANCES, YOU MUST DECLARE THE GOODS IN THE RED CHANNEL. IF YOU DO NOT, YOU ARE BREAKING THE LAW AND WE MAY PROSECUTE YOU.

4 HOW TO GO THROUGH CUSTOMS

Use the RED CHANNEL if you:
- have goods to declare
- are not sure what you should declare

5

Use the GREEN CHANNEL if you are travelling from a NON-EU COUNTRY, with:
- no more than the customs allowance

6

Use the BLUE CHANNEL if you are travelling from an EU COUNTRY, with:
- no tobacco products that are over the limits for imports from that country

3 **Look at the parts of the customs guide which are about what you can bring in. Complete the sentences.**

a Part(s) .... is/are for people travelling from the European Union (EU).

b Part(s) .... is/are for people who are not travelling from the European Union (EU).

4 **Complete these sentences about yourself.**

I'm from .... (name of country).

Part(s) .... is/are most useful to me.

Focus on ... ab©def

must, mustn't and _don't have to_

Complete these expressions from the text.

a you .... pay any tax

b you .... sell these goods

c you .... declare the goods in the Red Channel

Match the verbs with their meanings.

d must — it is necessary not to

e mustn't — it is necessary to

f don't have to — it isn't necessary to

Complete these sentences with _must_, _mustn't_ or _don't have to_. You will need to read the guide again.

g You .... declare gifts worth less than £145.

h You .... bring in the maximum allowance for both cigarettes and cigars.

i You .... declare any goods that are over the allowances.

j If you bring in alcohol, this .... be for a commercial purpose.

---

5 **Answer these questions.**

a Why don't people coming from the EU pay tax on goods when they arrive in the UK?

....

b Which goods don't people coming from outside the EU pay tax on?

....

6 **Look at the parts which are about how you should go through Customs. Complete these sentences.**

a People from the European Union should use the .... customs channel – if ....

....

b Other people should use the ....

....

....

7 **Read about these travellers. Which customs channel should these people go through? Complete the chart.**

Person	Travelling from	Products	Channel
Cintia	Brazil	1 litre of spirits + 2 litres of sparkling wine	red
Daisuke	Japan	30cc of perfume + 150cc of eau de toilette	
Zofia	Poland	25 cigars as a birthday present	
Christian	Sweden	a new digital camera + an iPod	

E✗tra practice

Check the customs regulations for your country on the Internet. What are the main differences from the UK regulations?

Can-do checklist

Tick what you can do.

	Can do	Need more practice
I can find words with similar meanings in a text.	✓	✓
I can find out about restrictions to my hand luggage.		
I can decide if I need to declare anything at Customs.		

Unit 5
Where shall we eat?

go to Useful language p. 83

Get ready to read

- Look at the food items. <u>Underline</u> the correct word in each pair.

a   b   c   d   e   f

a garlic / <u>pepper</u>
b onion / asparagus
c olives / grapes
d artichoke / orange
e cucumber / melon
f lemon / lettuce

- Match these food specialities with the countries they are from. Have you ever tried any of these specialities?

a tempura
b Quiche Lorraine
c Baklava
d Peking duck
e Nasi goreng
f Enchiladas
g Tabbouleh
h Wiener schnitzel

1 Austria
2 China
3 France
4 Indonesia
5 Japan
6 Lebanon
7 Mexico
8 Turkey

- You are going to read about eating out in Andalucia – an area in southern Spain. Have you ever eaten Spanish food? How many Spanish dishes can you name?

A I'd like to try that

1 You have just arrived in Andalucia and you are looking at the food section of your guidebook. <u>Underline</u> the words you would NOT expect to find in a text about food and eating out.

ingredients	speciality	savoury	slice	grilled
batter	mixture	beach	order	trees

2 Scan the text and <u>underline</u> the words from Exercise 1. (The words in the text do not always appear in the same form as in Exercise 1.)

3 Look at the pictures on the opposite page. Match them with the specialities mentioned in the text. Write the numbers in the boxes.

a *Patatas bravas* [7]
b *Tortilla Española* [ ]
c *Gazpacho* [ ]
d *Calamares* [ ]
e *Arroz a la marinera* [ ]
f Salads [ ]
g Olive oil [ ]

4 Read about each speciality. <u>Underline</u> all the ingredients. (Not every speciality contains ingredients.)

Eating out in Andalucia

Local ingredients are of a fantastic quality and this is the secret of Andalucian cooking. Here are some of the specialities of the region.

Patatas bravas and *Tortilla Española*
Both of these dishes are very popular, not just in Andalucia, but all over Spain. The first consists of fried potatoes which are served with a spicy sauce. The second is a heavy potato omelette with onions, fried into a savoury cake. It is served either hot or cold by the slice and is so filling that it can make a full meal.

Gazpacho
This favourite Andalucian dish is a cold soup made of fresh tomatoes, green peppers, cucumber, garlic, olive oil, lemon, breadcrumbs and salt. There are lots of local variations, which may include almonds, grapes, melon, red peppers, and boiled egg garnishes.

Calamares
All along the coast you will find grilled baby squid – whole squid are simple and delicious, as long as they are fresh. A common alternative is to cut them into rings and fry them in batter – again, if they are fresh, they will taste sweet and tender.

Arroz a la marinera
This is rice served with a mixture of shellfish – it is the Andalucian version of paella. Unlike the traditional paella from Valencia, *arroz a la marinera* does not contain any chicken or sausage. A very good choice for lunch in a beach restaurant!

Focus on ...
vocabulary

a You can cook food items in the following ways: *bake, boil, fry, grill, roast*. Scan the text for one of these words and for three related words which end in –*ed*. Underline the words in the text.

b Which ways can you cook these things?

	bake	boil	fry	grill	roast
eggs					
chicken					
rice					
bread					

c Choose three other food items and write them in the chart. Which ways can you cook these things?

	bake	boil	fry	grill	roast

Salads

Andalucian salads are large and often come with asparagus, hard-boiled eggs, tuna, artichoke, olives and onions, in addition to lettuce and tomato. You can ask for any of these ingredients to be left off your order if you prefer. Málaga salad is a delicious mixture of small pieces of cod, boiled potato, oranges, green olives and onion, dressed with good olive oil. Salads are very healthy too!

Olive oil

Olive oil is one of the main ingredients of the Andalucian diet. Spain is the biggest producer of olive oil in the world and half of its production comes from Andalucia. Olive trees were first introduced to the area more than three thousand years ago by the Phoenicians, who began exporting olive oil to other parts of the Mediterranean. Why not try rubbing a piece of toast with garlic and then pouring olive oil onto it? It makes a wonderful breakfast!

5 **Read the text again. Decide if these sentences are true (T) or false (F).**

a *Patatas bravas* is eaten throughout Spain. ..T..
b *Tortilla* is always eaten cold. ......
c *Gazpacho* is always made from almonds and grapes. ......
d Squid can be eaten whole or cut into rings. ......
e There isn't any meat in *arroz a la marinera*. ......
f Andalucian salads usually include lettuce and tomato. ......
g Lots of olives are grown in Andalucia. ......

Learning tip

Our purpose in reading a text is to understand the writer's message. This means understanding the words the writer uses and also understanding what the writer wants to do with these words. They could be giving an instruction, presenting facts, giving the writer's opinion, etc. Understanding a text requires us to work out the *function* of each sentence.

6 **Look at the sentences in Exercise 5 again. Are these about facts or opinions?**

7 **Read the section *Arroz a la marinera* again. Read each sentence carefully and work out its function. Complete the chart.**

Sentence 1	Sentence 2	Sentence 3	
✓			describes the dish/ingredient
			gives other facts about it
			recommends the dish or makes a suggestion

8 **Read the last two sections of the text. Work out the function of each sentence as in Exercise 7. Make and complete two charts similar to the one above.**

9 **Would you follow any of the author's recommendations? Which dish(es) would you most like to try?**

B This looks good

1 When you are choosing a place to eat, which of these things are important to you? Put them in order. (1 = most important, 5 = least important)

a location of the restaurant/café ☐
b price ☐
c size of the dishes ☐
d service ☐
e the menu ☐

2 Skim these messages from a website about eating out in Seville, the largest city in Andalucia. Did the people who wrote the messages like the places they reviewed, or not? Put a tick ✓ or a cross ✗ next to each restaurant.

Did you know …?

Seville is the English name for the Spanish city *Sevilla*. This is the only Spanish city that has a different name in English. On the other hand, several Italian city names (*Roma, Venezia, Firenze*, etc.) have different names in English (*Rome, Venice, Florence*, etc.).

Seville eating out

a

Las Coloniales

Posted by Tobias 14 September

The *tapas* (bar snacks) here are enormous, which means you can eat very cheaply. You could easily have a good meal with a drink for €5.
My favourite dish is *pollo con salsa de almendra* (chicken in almond sauce) and I also love their *champiñones rebozados* (fried mushrooms stuffed with ham and sausage). They also do lots of grilled fish and meat.

If you want to eat outside, you will need to get here early – this is a very popular place – and write your name on the chalk board. The restaurant is at Plaza Cristo de Burgos, 19. The square has quite a few trees so you can get some shade while you wait for your table. There's also a wonderful *heladeria* (café selling ice cream) nearby and the square gets very busy on Sunday afternoons when Spanish families visit. You might want to go there yourself – this *heladeria* (I can't remember its name) is expensive, but it's got the best ice cream I've tasted in Seville. (Plaza Cristo de Burgos is just past Plaza de Encarnación and east of the main El Corte Inglés department store.)

Seville | eating | bar | family | budget
100% agreed
12 people

b

El Faro de Triana

Posted by AMcL 15 November

It is worth going to El Faro (lighthouse) for the views alone. It's right next to the river on the Triana side, at the end of the Puente Isabel II (Isabel II bridge). (Locals call this the Puente de Triana.) Also it's on four floors. From a table on the rooftop terrace, you get a fantastic view towards the bullring and the cathedral. It's easy to get a table on the terrace at lunchtime, but you'll soon find out why – the sun can burn you at this time of day.

El Faro is famous for its fish and seafood. The *gambas* (prawns) and *pescado frito* (mixed fried fish) are highly recommended – we shared a plate of fish and it was big enough for two.

Seville | eating | bar | family | budget
80% agreed
4 people

c

El Cordobes

Posted by Isabel 2 November

The *menu del día* (menu of the day) is very good value and you can have it at any time of day. The menu is advertised at €7 and that's what you pay. There are no additional charges – unlike some other places I've been to.

El Cordobes is in Santa María la Blanca, a busy square in the Santa Cruz area. You can either eat inside or out. I prefer to sit outside under the orange trees.

Seville | eating | bar | family | budget
50% agreed
8 people

d

Il Vesuvio

Posted by jessiec 16 October

I don't want Spanish food every day of the week and Il Vesuvio was exactly what I was looking for. Italian food is usually great and here it's very reasonably priced and very fresh too. I loved this restaurant so much that I went there four times in a week.

Il Vesuvio is at Calle Tetuán, 15 (Pasaje de las Delicias) in the main central shopping district and it's easy to find. It's open every day from 12.30pm–4.30pm and 8pm–1am. You don't need to book a table in advance, but the phone number is 954 77 83 just in case.

Seville | eating | Italian
40% agreed
6 people

3 **Read the messages again. Did each reviewer mention features a–e in Exercise 1? What did they say about them? Complete the chart where possible. (Not every reviewer mentions every feature.)**

	Location of the restaurant/café	Price	Size of the dishes	Service	Menu
Message a	Plaza Cristo de Burgos, 19, near a shop selling ice-cream				
Message b					
Message c					
Message d					

4 **Two of the messages mention other places to eat in Seville. Which messages, and which places do they mention? What do they say about them? Complete the sentences.**

a Message _____ mentions _____

_____

b Message _____ mentions _____

_____

5 **Other people have read the reviews. Did they agree with them? Match the beginnings and endings of these sentences.**

Half the people   agreed with message a.
Over three-quarters of the people   agreed with message b.
All the people   agreed with message c.
More than a third of the people   agreed with message d.

6 **Which restaurant would you try first? Why?**

Class bonus

Choose one of the restaurants. Imagine you went there last night. Write a short note to a friend about your evening. Read out your note to the class. How many people were at the same restaurant?

E X tra practice

Look on the Internet and find other recommendations for restaurants in Seville. You could try www.exploreseville.com. Would you like to go to these restaurants?

Can-do checklist

Tick what you can do.

	Can do	Need more practice
I can understand descriptions of dishes and recommendations, and choose what I would like to eat.	✔	✔
I can work out the function of each sentence in a text.		
I can understand web recommendations and choose a place to eat.		

Unit6
Somewhere to stay

Get ready to read

- Where can you stay when you go on holiday?
  Write five types of holiday accommodation.

  bed and breakfast _____ ☐

  _____ ☐

  _____ ☐

  _____ ☐

  _____ ☐

  _____ ☐

- Which of these things can you usually do in a hotel? Put a tick ✓ or a cross ✗.
  a You can have a private bathroom. ☑
  b You can cook your own meals. ☐
  c You can wash your clothes. ☐
  d You can have breakfast in your room. ☐
  e You can watch TV in your room. ☐
  f You can pay by credit card. ☐

- Tick ✓ the types of accommodation above that you have stayed in.

go to Useful language p. 83

A Banff Y Mountain Lodge

1 **In this unit, you are going to read about some holiday accommodation in Banff, Canada. Skim the webpage. What kind of accommodation does it describe?**

_____

Did you know ...?

Canada is the second largest country after Russia, but its population is less than 30 million. 34% of its people are British in origin and 26% are French. Canada has two official languages – English and French. Most French speakers live in Quebec province. Banff is in the Rocky Mountains.

File   Edit   View   Favorites   Tools   Help

Address   http://www.hostelbookers.com/hostels/canada/banff/6082   ⌄ → Go   Links »

hostelbookers.com
Great Hostels. Free Booking. No Worries.
Hostelbookers ▶ All hostels ▶ Canada ▶ Banff ▶ Banff Y Mountain Lodge

Banff Y Mountain Lodge
102 Spray Avenue, Banff, AB, T1L 1A6, Canada - map - directions

Welcome! We are among huge pine trees right next to the Bow River, yet close to downtown Banff. Make us your home away from home for any reason in any season.

✔ 24-hour hot showers	✔ Credit cards accepted	✔ Self-catering facilities
✔ No curfew	✔ Internet	✔ Lounge area
✔ Safety deposit	✔ Washing machines	✔ Restaurant

Overall ratings – as reviewed by Hostelbookers customers

Atmosphere	77%	Fun	73%	Safety	88%
Location	95%	Staff	83%	Value	88%
Facilities	83%	Cleanliness	87%		

overall average
84.4%

We offer private and dormitory rooms for budget travellers and short-term residents, and are open to women, men, families and all types of group.

We also offer internet kiosks, and kitchen and laundry facilities for your convenience.

Shared from 31.00*   Private from 75.00*
*all prices in Canadian dollars
Hostel features

Rating ✔ 84.4%	Bed linen ✔ free	Airport pickup ✗ not included
Breakfast ✗ not included	Towel ✔ free	Luggage Room ✗ not included

Learning tip

Before you read a text, think about the topic – either in your own language or in English. Use your knowledge and experience to try and predict what the text – the whole text and/or parts of it – will say. You probably won't be able to predict the exact words, but it will help you understand the text if you can predict the kind of thing it will say.

2 Before you read the webpage more carefully, think about what you expect to find in this type of accommodation. Which of the things (a–f) in *Get ready to read* can you usually do in this type of accommodation?

----

3 Write down three other things you can do in this type of accommodation.

----

4 Look at the icons. Match them with the nine blue ticked ✓ features of the hostel.

a   <u>Washing machines</u>   f   ------------------
b   ------------------   g   ------------------
c   ------------------   h   ------------------
d   ------------------   i   ------------------
e   ------------------

5 Choose the two most important and the two least important features for you.

most important   ☐ and ☐
least important   ☐ and ☐

6 Backpackers can rate (= judge the quality of) each Hostelbookers hostel. They judge the quality of eight aspects of the hostel by giving a percentage (%). <u>Underline</u> the eight aspects on the website.

Focus on ...
vocabulary

Read these comments that guests of the Banff Y Mountain Lodge have made. Complete the comments with some of the eight words you <u>underlined</u> in Exercise 6.

a   'The people who worked there were wonderful. Full marks to the ____<u>staff</u>____ !'
b   'I have no complaints about _____ . I didn't see any dirt anywhere.'
c   'This hostel is great _____ for money. It's only 75 dollars for a private room.'
d   'The _____ of this hostel is wonderful. It's very easy to get to.'
e   'The other people in my room were great. In fact, everyone was very friendly and relaxed. There was a really good _____ !'
f   'I met a great group of people and had a lot of _____ here.'

7 Look at the overall ratings for this hostel on the webpage. Which aspect of the hostel did guests like the most? <u>Underline</u> more information on the webpage about this aspect.

----

8 Read these questions that guests ask about the hostel. Then scan the rest of the webpage and answer the questions. Answer *yes* or *no*.

a   Do all beds in shared rooms cost $31 per night?   ----*no*----

b   Can I have a room of my own?   ----------

c   Can families use the hostel?   ----------

d   Is breakfast included in the price?   ----------

d   Do I have to have my own sleeping bag?   ----------

f   Do I have to pay to leave my backpack in a safe place?   ----------

9 What other questions would you ask when finding out about staying in a hostel? (The answers to your questions do not need to be in the text.)

B Frequently Asked Questions

1 Look at the website in Section A again. How do you think you book accommodation at Banff Y Mountain Lodge?

2 Here are three FAQs (Frequently Asked Questions) from another webpage on the Hostelbookers website. Read the answers from Hostelbookers. Is the short answer to each question *yes* or *no*?

a ....
b ....
c ....

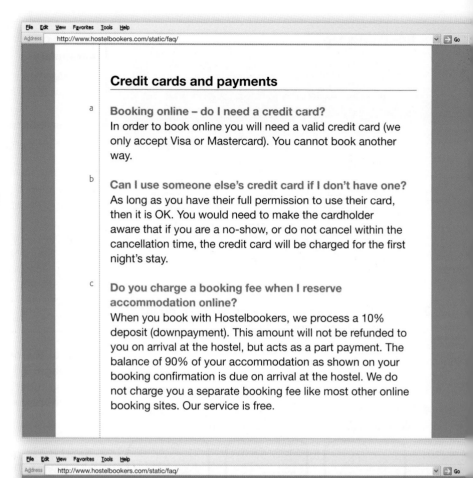

File Edit View Favorites Tools Help

Address http://www.hostelbookers.com/static/faq/   Go

Credit cards and payments

a **Booking online – do I need a credit card?**
In order to book online you will need a valid credit card (we only accept Visa or Mastercard). You cannot book another way.

b **Can I use someone else's credit card if I don't have one?**
As long as you have their full permission to use their card, then it is OK. You would need to make the cardholder aware that if you are a no-show, or do not cancel within the cancellation time, the credit card will be charged for the first night's stay.

c **Do you charge a booking fee when I reserve accommodation online?**
When you book with Hostelbookers, we process a 10% deposit (downpayment). This amount will not be refunded to you on arrival at the hostel, but acts as a part payment. The balance of 90% of your accommodation as shown on your booking confirmation is due on arrival at the hostel. We do not charge you a separate booking fee like most other online booking sites. Our service is free.

3 Here are some more FAQs from the webpage. You probably do not know the answers, but what do you *think* the answers to questions (a–k) could be? Some answers are simply *yes* or *no*; others are longer.

> **Class bonus**
>
> Discuss your answers with a partner before reading the website answers. Are your ideas similar or different?

File Edit View Favorites Tools Help

Address http://www.hostelbookers.com/static/faq/   Go

FAQs (Frequently Asked Questions)

Booking online
a Can I book over the telephone or by email?
b Do I need to be a member of any hostel or youth organisation to book?
c Do I need to book in advance?
d Can you give me directions and contact details of a hostel before I book?

Your booking
e What do I do if I make a mistake in my booking?
f Do I receive confirmation after I book?
g Can I cancel a booking or change my booking on Hostelbookers?

In the hostel
h Do the hostels have age restrictions or limitations?
i What does 'Private room' mean?
j What is a dormitory room?
k What does 'en suite' mean?

4 Skim the answers to the FAQs below. Match the questions on the opposite page with the answers.

a [2]   b ☐   c ☐   d ☐   e ☐   f ☐   g ☐   h ☐   i ☐   j ☐   k ☐

File   Edit   View   Favorites   Tools   Help

Address   http://www.hostelbookers.com/static/faq/   ✔ → Go   Links »

¹ This is a room that is not shared with other people from the hostel, in other words not communal. A private double room has a double bed. Private twin rooms have two single beds.

² We can only process online reservations through our website, www.hostelbookers.com. All of our availability is shown there.

³ If you have accidentally made a mistake in your booking, whether it's booking the wrong rooms or the wrong dates, you do not have to rebook, just contact the hostel and change your booking with them.

⁴ We would recommend that you book far in advance in order to avoid disappointment and to make sure you get a bed at the hostel you would like to stay at. Many hostels are booked up well in advance during high season, weekends, holiday periods or during special events.

⁵ If you have an en suite room, this means that this room has basic shower and toilet facilities inside of the room. If the rooms have en suites, it would specify on the room description, e.g. Private twin en suite. If it does not have an en suite, it will state, e.g. Private twin.

⁶Yes, we provide the address on our website. Unfortunately we are not able to provide telephone details for the hostels, but once you have made a booking and you receive confirmation, you will be provided with contact details in order to contact them for directions.

⁷ No, you do not need to be a member of any youth hostel organisation to book at any of the hostels listed on Hostelbookers.

⁸ Yes, you do receive a confirmation from us, showing the amount that you have paid and the outstanding amount that still needs to be paid upon arrival. The hostel's contact details are on the confirmation in case you need to contact them.

⁹ This is a shared room. Most dormitories have 4 beds, 6 beds or 8 beds, and some are larger. Some hostels have males-only dorms and females-only dorms or mixed. By booking a dorm with your friends this may mean that you are not in the same room.

¹⁰ No, if you need to cancel or amend your booking, you would need to contact the hostel and do so directly with them. We are not able to do this for you. In the event of a cancellation, you need to give 48 hours notice, or the hostel will charge you for the first night's stay (though we suggest checking the hostel's special terms before booking as these may differ). In any cancellation or amendment, please be aware that the deposit is non-refundable.

¹¹ This can change from hostel to hostel. Most hostels will accept any guest between the ages of 18 and 35. Some hostels will take under 18s, but you have to be accompanied by an adult and stay in a Private room.

5 Read the answers carefully. How many answers in Exercise 3 did you guess correctly?

6 Are there any other questions you would like to ask about Hostelbookers? Write two more questions.

E✗tra practice

Look on the Hostelbookers website www.hostelbookers.com, and try and find the answers to the questions you asked in Exercise 6.

Can-do checklist

Tick what you can do.

	Can do	Need more practice
I can use my knowledge and experience to predict the content of a text.	✔	✔
I can find out about a hostel and what it offers.		
I can find the answers to frequently asked questions.		

Get ready to read

○ Which of these sentences are true for you? Put a tick ✓ for true sentences or a cross ✗ for false.

I've been in a cable car. (There is one in the photos on these pages.) ☐

I'm not afraid of heights. ☐

I don't like walking up mountains. ☐

I like walking down mountains. ☐

○ Where do you usually do these things? Tick ✓ the correct place in the chart.

	Bottom of cableway	Top of cableway
a buy a ticket		
b get a good view		
c check the time of the last cable car		
d take some photos		
e have a drink or something to eat		
f go for a walk		

go to Useful language p. 84

A Table Mountain Cableway

1 **Imagine you are having breakfast in your hotel in Cape Town in South Africa. It is a wonderful day with clear blue skies. You pick up a leaflet in your hotel. Skim the front of the leaflet and answer the questions.**

a What can you see on the front of the leaflet?

----

b Would today be a good day for this trip?

----

2 **Scan the front of the leaflet. Which of these things is the leaflet going to tell you about? Put a tick ✓ or a cross ✗.**

a somewhere to buy things ✓

b the price of tickets ☐

c somewhere to eat ☐

d the opening hours of the cableway ☐

e somewhere to have a drink in the evening ☐

Did you know …?

The *rand* (R) is the currency of South Africa. There are 100 *cents* in one *rand*.

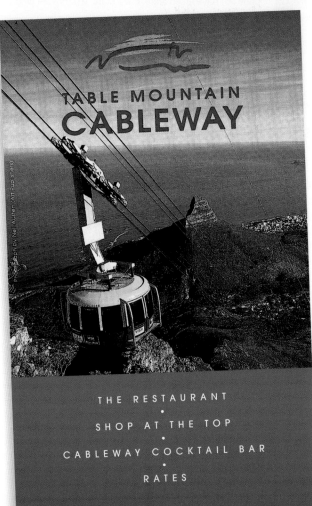

TABLE MOUNTAIN
CABLEWAY

THE RESTAURANT
·
SHOP AT THE TOP
·
CABLEWAY COCKTAIL BAR
·
RATES

3 Now scan the inside of the leaflet. Does the leaflet tell you about the other thing in Exercise 2?

4 You are not sure whether to do this trip immediately. Find the answers to these questions.

   a What's the last time you can go up in the cable car?

   ----

   b How much will a normal return ticket cost?

   ----

5 You notice that you can buy a one-way ticket. What does this suggest you can do from the top?

6 You are interested in buying a souvenir of Table Mountain. Tick ✓ the part of the text which is most likely to tell you about buying souvenirs.

CABLEWAY CATERING SELF-SERVICE RESTAURANT

The self-service restaurant offers a full breakfast and an extensive hot and cold buffet.
Internet facilities and coin-operated telephones are available. The restaurant is situated on the top of Table Mountain and directions can be found as you make your way to the top.

WINTER RATES
1ST MAY 2004 - 15TH SEPTEMBER 2004

Adults:	Return	R 80.00
	One Way	R 44.00
Children: (under 18 years)	Return	R 44.00
	One Way	R 22.00
SA Senior Residents: (Over the age of 60 years with SA ID.)	Return	R 44.00
	One Way	R 22.00
Students: (With valid student card)	Return	R 60.00
	One Way	R 31.00
Family Ticket: (2 adults, 2 children U18)	Return	R 210.00

CABLEWAY CURIOS SHOP AT THE TOP GIFTS AND CURIOS

Shop at the Top is situated in the original stone cottage and offers visitors a wide range of merchandise bearing the insignia of South Africa's premier tourist attraction, Table Mountain.

- Tourist information available
- Exclusive Cableway clothing and gifts
- Film and stamps available
- All major Visa & Mastercards welcome

CABLEWAY OPENING TIMES
WINTER SEASON

First car up: 08h30
Last car up: 17h00
Last car down: 18h00

♿ **Need help?** Ask any staff member for assistance

CABLEWAY CATERING THE CABLEWAY COCKTAIL BAR

Welcome to Table Top Mountain Aerial Cableway, part of the Table Mountain National Park.

Enjoy the views of the city and Robben Island from the highest point on Table Mountain. Sunset cocktails and full bar facilities are available. The Cableway Cocktail Bar can be found inside the top cable station.

Learning tip

When you come across an unknown word, don't stop. Continue reading and – if you think it is an important word – come back to it later. Try and work out its meaning. Decide whether the word is an adjective, noun, verb, etc. Think about similar words in your own language and similar words in English. Look for any examples which illustrate the unknown word. Look at any pictures for help. Look for a word you know within the word. Also, the context – the words around the unknown word – should help you to try and work out its meaning. Ask yourself: What could this word mean here? You might not be able to work out the exact meaning of a word, but you will probably have a good idea.

7 Underline the words *cottage*, *merchandise*, *insignia* and *exclusive* in the leaflet. If you do not know their meaning, try to work it out. Use these questions to help you.

   a *cottage*: What kind of things can be made of stone? Does the picture help?

   b *merchandise*: What do shops usually sell? Find examples of merchandise in the list of points.

   c *insignia*: Look inside the word for another word. Could *insignia* be some kind of sign or symbol? Look at both the front and the inside of the leaflet and see if you can find one.

   d *exclusive*: Do you think you can buy these things at any other place in Cape Town?

8 Would you like to go up Table Mountain? Would you like to buy a souvenir?

E ✗tra practice

The leaflet mentions Robben Island. What do you know about Robben Island? Find out about it in a guidebook or on the Internet. Would you like to go there?

B The cable cars

1 Scan the two sides of this ticket for the Table Mountain cable car. What date and what time did the person buy the ticket?

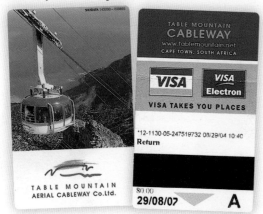

Did you know ...?

Notice the way in which the date is written in two different ways on the ticket – once with the month before the day and once with the day before the month. In Britain, people write the day before the month; in the US, they write the month before the day.

UK	US
10.1.08	1.10.08

You say this date in two ways:
The tenth of January, two thousand and eight.
January the tenth, two thousand and eight.

2 You pick up another leaflet about Table Mountain when you buy your ticket. Skim the leaflet quickly. Which two parts of the leaflet are about the cable cars? What is the other part about? Complete these sentences.

   a Parts _____ and _____ are about the cable cars.
   b Part _____ is about _____

3 A friend has already told you that you can have a 360° view from the cable car. How is this possible? <u>Underline</u> the answer in the first part of the leaflet. Ignore any other unknown words – they are not important to you in this exercise.

4 You have bought your ticket. It is a bit windy at the bottom of the cableway. Why don't you need to worry about this? <u>Underline</u> the answer in parts 1 and 2 of the leaflet. Again, ignore any unknown words.

1
Table Mountain Rotair
Information guide
www.tablemountain.net

TABLE MOUNTAIN AERIAL CABLEWAY Co. Ltd.

Welcome

The Rotair Aerial Cableway has been in operation since October 1997. The 65-passenger cable car runs from Cape Town to the top of the famous Table Mountain.

The round form of the Rotair cabin fulfils two functions: first, thanks to the revolving floor, passengers can enjoy the 360° degree panoramic view. Second it is aerodynamic in high winds. In these instances, the filled water tank in the floor of the cabin offers additional weight and stability. During normal weather, the tank is emptied at the upper station and the water is supplied to the restaurant.

Focus on ...
vocabulary   ab c def

Complete these sentences with words from the sentences you read in Exercises 3 and 4.

   a If a shop has ____revolving____ doors, people can usually only enter one at a time.
   b We had a _____ view of the city from the top floor of our hotel.
   c If something has a shape that moves easily through air, it is _____ .
   d The government used to change frequently, but now we have political _____ .
   e The Italian paintings are on the _____ floors of the gallery.
   f If you take a trip in a balloon, there will probably be sandbags used for _____ .

Class bonus

How much can you remember about the cable cars? Play a memory game. Take turns to make one sentence each. Don't repeat anything that another student has already said.

2
About the Cable Car

- The cable cars have a carrying capacity of 65 people. 900 people per hour

- Speed: maximum of 10 metres per second

- The lengths of the cables are 1 200m

- The cables weigh 18 tonnes

- The height of Table Mountain at its highest point is 1 085m

- The cable car can carry a weight of 5 200 kg

- The cable cars carry 4 000 litres of water used for ballast during the windy season; they also provide fresh water for visitors

- The cableway works on a counter weight system weighing 134 tonnes each

3
Table Mountain Aerial Cableway's main environmental concerns are to:

1 Conserve the biodiversity of Table Mountain
2 Prevent the degradation of the environment
3 Minimise water consumption
4 Reduce damage caused by visitors
5 Lower the visual impact of TMACC facilities

Please help us by:

- Not littering
- Not damaging or chipping the rocks
- Not feeding the animals
- Not picking the flowers
- Not wasting water
- Staying on the footpaths
- Smoking in designated areas only

Smoking is not permitted on the footpaths as it is a fire hazard and a major source of litter.

For more info on Table Mountain Cableway
Phone: (021) 424 8181
Fax: (021) 424 3792
website: www.tablemountain.net

---

5 **Look at part 3 of the leaflet. Try and work out the meaning of the following words.**

   a *biodiversity*: This refers to the different (or *diverse*) types of what? Find two words in the section 'Please help us by' .... , ...

   b *degradation*: Find a word in the same section with a similar meaning. ....

   c *minimize*: Find two words in the same section with a similar meaning. .... , ...

6 **Read the three parts of the text again without focusing on any unknown words. Use a pencil to quickly <u>underline</u> any words you do not understand.**

7 **Read the text again. Try and work out the meaning of the words you underlined.**

Can-do checklist

Tick what you can do.

	Can do	Need more practice
I can read and find the information I need without focusing on unknown words.	✓	✓
I can try and work out the meaning of unknown words.		✓
I can find out about an attraction from leaflets about it.		

Unit8
It's ringing

Get ready to read

- ⊙ Circle one of the verbs and complete the sentence so that it is true for you.
  I *need* / *don't need* a mobile phone because

- ⊙ Tick ✓ the options that are true for you.
  I use my mobile phone:
  all the time ☐
  for emergencies only ☐
  to text people ☐
  to receive calls only ☐

  At home, I use:
  my landline ('home' phone) ☐
  my mobile phone ☐

  For my mobile phone, I pay:
  for each call I make ☐
  a fixed amount every month ☐

go to Useful language p. 84

A Three great packages

1 **Read the questions below and try to work out the meaning of the words in *italics*. Then answer the questions by <u>underlining</u> the part of the sentence which is true for you.**

a Do you call your friends or do you *text* them?

b Do you buy CDs or do you *download* music from the Internet?

c Did you buy your computer and screen separately or as a *package*?

d Do you pay each time you go online, or do you have *unlimited* access to the Internet for a fixed fee?

e Are your friends on the same mobile phone *network* as you or are they on a different one?

f Have you thought about getting *broadband* or have you already got it?

g Do you speak to your friends on your mobile or on a *landline*?

h Do you speak to your friends during the day or only at *off-peak* times?

2 **You are thinking about changing your mobile phone package. Scan the brochure on the oposite page about *Pay monthly*. Who are the three options for and why is each mobile good for that type of person? Complete the sentences.**

1 ____Dolphin____ is for people who __text a lot__ .
  They will get _____
  _____
  _____
  _____ .

2 _____ is for people who _____ .
  They will get _____
  _____
  _____
  _____ .

3 _____ is for people who _____ .
  They will get _____
  _____
  _____
  _____ .

Learning tip

When you read a text which compares similar things, use a chart to record the most important points for comparison. This type of note-taking helps to simplify the information in the text.

pay monthly

three great packages to give you exactly what you need

1

text a lot?

If you like to text a lot, Dolphin is for you. You'll get loads of inclusive texts, plus free downloads to personalise your phone.
So, if you prefer texting over talking, Dolphin is the package for you.

Available in £19, £25 and £35 packages.

unlimited texts
500 cross network minutes
unlimited free calls to your Magic Number*
(add a new Magic Number every six months)
4 free downloads
every month on Dolphin £35
PLUS
free broadband

2

call landlines a lot?

If you want no-nonsense basics and see your phone as a tool not a toy, Racoon is for you. You'll get extra minutes to standard UK landlines, plus Answer Phone is included too.
So, if you call landlines a lot, Racoon is the package for you.

Available in £25, £30 and £35 packages.

unlimited landline calls
500 cross network minutes
200 texts
unlimited free calls to your Magic Number*
(add a new Magic Number every six months)
free traffic TV for three months
free Answer Phone
every month on Racoon £35
PLUS
free broadband

3

talk a lot off-peak?

If you want more minutes to catch up with friends and family, Canary is for you. You'll get extra minutes to chirp away through the night and all weekend long.
So, if you make most of your calls in the evenings and at weekends, Canary is the package for you.

Available in £30 and £40 packages.

unlimited Orange off-peak minutes
600 cross network minutes
400 texts
unlimited free calls to your Magic Number*
(add a new Magic Number every six months)
free Orange photography for three months
every month on Canary £40
PLUS
free broadband

*When you join Orange on an 18-month contract and choose an Orange number as your Magic Number, you can make unlimited free calls to that number.

3 Scan the brochure and complete the chart.

	Maximum monthly cost	Cross network minutes every month	Texts every month	Type of extra minutes free every month
Dolphin	£35			–
Racoon				
Canary				

4 Look at the text again. Which two things do all three packages offer?

5 What extras does each package offer? Complete the sentences.
  a Dolphin offers _____ and _____ .
  b Racoon offers _____ .
  c Canary offers _____ .

6 Which package would you choose? Why?

Class bonus

Choose one of the packages and describe it to another student. Include one extra piece of information – or one piece of information that is incorrect. Can your friend identify the extra piece of information or mistake?

E✗tra practice

Find out about another mobile phone package by visiting the website of a mobile phone provider you know. How does this package compare with the three you have already read about?

B How much will it cost?

1 An American friend is visiting your country. He does not want to use his mobile phone because it is too expensive. Answer his questions (if you can).

a Which coins do I need for calls from a public phone box?

----

b Can I dial the US direct or must I phone the operator?

----

c Can I pay by credit card if I phone the US?

----

d What's the international code for this country?

----

e What is the number for the emergency services?

----

f What is the number for directory enquiries?

----

2 You have lost your mobile phone and you need to make some calls from a public phone box in London. You are worried about how much calls might cost. Skim the phone box notice on the right and complete the sentence with the correct section numbers.

Sections .... and .... are about paying for calls.

---

[1] Telephone prices

Coins – From 16th November the minimum fee is 40p (includes 20p connection charge). Local & National* calls are charged at 40p for the first 20 minutes, then 10p for each subsequent 10 minutes or portion thereof.

Payment by Euro – Minimum fee 1 Euro. Length of call depends on current exchange rate. For the current rate of exchange for Euro used in this payphone, please call 100 and request the BT Payphones Customer Services Team.

Credit / Debit cards – 20p per minute. Minimum fee £1.20 (includes £1 connection charge) for Local and National* calls.

Please call 100 amd request the BT Payphones Customer Services Team for current prices for your call.

*Excludes non-geographic numbers (e.g. 0845, 0870), Directory Enquiries calls, calls to premium rate numbers, mobile phones, international numbers, personal numbering, paging services and calls made via the Operator. Other restrictions apply.

[2] Payment

Accepted payment methods may vary between payphones. Coin accepting payphones accept 10p, 20p, 50p & £1 coins. Some coin accepting payphones accept £2 coins. Some coin accepting payphones accept 50c and 1 Euro coins, some also accept 2 Euro coins. Euro coins can only be used for directly dialled calls. Payphones operate and display in £ sterling. See the payphone display for details.

Where coins are accepted, only unused coins will be returned. For short calls avoid using 50p, £1, £2, and 2 Euro coins.

Calls to Emergency Services and freephone numbers are free. Incoming calls accepted.

Calls using a Credit/Debit Card – To make a call using a Credit/Debit Card, please swipe the card through the card reader and follow the instructions. If there is no card reader on this phone, please call 0800 032 0023 and follow the voice prompts to complete the call.

[3] International codes

Australia 00 61+	Germany 00 49+	Italy 00 39+	Poland 00 48+
Bangladesh 00 880+	India 00 91+	Netherlands 00 31+	Spain 00 34+
France 00 33+	Ireland Republic 00 353+	Pakistan 00 92+	USA 00 1+

[4] How to contact BT

Free Operator assistance

Free Fault reporting

This phone works with a behind the ear hearing aid set to T.

UK 100
International 155
Payphones 151
Residential 151
Business 154

[5] BT Payphones Directory Enquiries

UK Inland 118 141 – Only available for cash calls.
Cash calls cost 70p for the first minute, then 50p per minute thereafter.

International 118 060 – Cash calls cost £2.20 for the first minute, then £2.00 per minute thereafter. Credit/Debit Card calls cost £3.00 for the first minute, then £2.00 per minute thereafter.

This phone is at
(020) 7839 3450 JCT ADELAIDE ST DUNCANNON ST, LONDON, WC2N 4JF

**SOS emergency calls –
dial 999 or 112 free**
For Police, Ambulance, Fire, Coastguard, Mountain Rescue and Cave Rescue

Samaritans 08567 90 90 90
Runaway Helpline 0808 800 70 70
Message Home Helpline 0800 700 740
Childline 0800 1111

Focus on ...
nouns and verbs

ab**c**def

Find the words *change* and *call* in the notice on the opposite page. (They both appear several times.) What are these words?

a nouns   b verbs   c both nouns and verbs

Complete these sentences from the notice. Are the missing words nouns (N) or verbs (V)? Circle the correct letter.

a Payphones operate and ___display___ in £ sterling.	N	Ⓥ
b See the payphone _____ for details.	N	V
c Cash calls _____ 70p for the first minute.	N	V
d This _____ is at (020) 7839 3450.	N	V
e SOS emergency calls – _____ 999 or 112 free	N	V

Complete these sentences with some of the words above. Are the missing words nouns (N) or verbs (V)?

f My parents ___call___ me every day when I'm away from home.	N	Ⓥ
g I usually _____ my friends in the evenings.	N	V
h BT don't _____ for reporting faults.	N	V
i The _____ of mobile phone packages is going down.	N	V
j Modern telephones don't have a _____ – they have buttons.	N	V

3 You want to phone a friend in London. What is the minimum cost of your call if you pay in the following ways? How long can you speak for? Complete the chart.

	Sterling coins	Euro coins	Credit card
minimum cost	40p		
length of call			

4 You want to phone a friend in Edinburgh – more than 500 kilometres away in Scotland. Would the call cost more than the call to your friend in Exercise 3?

5 You want to phone a friend in Florence, Italy. What information does the notice give you about the minimum cost of your call? Tick ✓ one of the boxes.

a The minimum cost is £1.20. ☐
b The minimum cost is £0.40. ☐
c The notice doesn't give this information. ☐

6 Imagine you have these coins in your wallet. Then answer the questions.

a Which ones are UK sterling?
b Which of the UK coins can you use in all public phones?
c When phones accept euros, can you use them for all types of call?
d If your call does not use all the money you put into the phone, what will you get back?
e If you haven't got enough money, can your friends call you back? What number should they use?

Did you know ...?

The *euro* (currency sign €) is the official currency of many European Union countries. *Euros* and *cents* were introduced in 2002 and replaced the Italian lira, Spanish peseta, etc. The currency of the UK is sterling (currency sign £). You can use euros in some British phones and shops (especially in London and at airports), but this is not common.

7 What advice would you give to your friends about paying for their calls?

Can-do checklist

Tick what you can do.

	Can do	Need more practice
I can use a chart to make notes and compare things.	✓	✓
I can choose the best mobile phone package for my needs.		
I can decide how to pay for calls from a public phone box.		

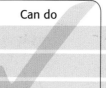

Unit 9
Don't worry!

Get ready to read

- Tick ✓ the sentences that are true for you.
  I've never cut myself badly. ☐
  I've never broken my leg. ☐
  I've never fallen and hit my head. ☐
  I've never helped someone in an emergency. ☐
  I've never been admitted to hospital and stayed overnight. ☐
  I've never done a first aid course. ☐

- Write two more sentences about accidents and first aid.
  I've never _broken my hand_ ....
  ....
  I've never ....
  ....

go to Useful language p. 84

A Cuts and grazes

1 Cilka is a nanny. She looks after two young children. One of the children has fallen on the pavement outside the house and hurt his knee. Cilka has got a first aid manual. Skim the page of the manual. Is this the page she should read?

2 Scan the page. One word is used many times instead of the nouns *cut* or *graze*. What is this word?

....

3 Which word is used to refer to the little boy who has hurt his knee?

....

Cuts and grazes

Small cuts and grazes soon stop bleeding without treatment. However, any break in the skin, even a small one, can allow germs to enter the body. Germs are micro-organisms, such as bacteria, that are carried by flies or by unwashed hands; if they are allowed to settle on an open wound, they can cause infection.

Your aims
▶ Stop wound from becoming infected
▶ Control any bleeding

You will need
▶ Disposable gloves
▶ Sterile gauze swabs or antiseptic wipes
▶ Plasters or sterile wound dressing
▶ Bandage

IMPORTANT
▶ Do not touch the open graze with your fingers while you are treating the casualty.
▶ Do not try to remove anything that is embedded in the wound.
▶ Do not use cotton wool on or near an open wound because fibres may stick to the wound.

1 Rinse wound

- Help the casualty to sit down.
- Put on disposable gloves, if available.
- Raise the injured part.
- Rinse the wound under cold running water to remove any dirt or grit.

2 Clean around the wound

- Using a fresh swab or wipe for each stroke, clean around the wound, working from the edge of the wound outwards.
- Carefully pick off any loose foreign matter, such as glass, metal, or gravel, from or around the wound.

3 Dry around wound

- Without disturbing the wound, gently dry the area around it with a gauze swab.

4 Cover wound

- For a small cut or graze, apply a plaster to the affected area; make sure you do not touch the sterile part of the plaster.
- If the cut or graze is too large for a plaster, cover it with a sterile wound dressing and secure the dressing with a bandage.
- Advise the casualty to rest the injured part and, if possible, to support it in a raised position.

4 **What are the four basic steps you should take to prevent a cut or graze from becoming infected? Complete the sentences.**

a You should _____rinse_____ it.

b You should ___bandage___ _____ it.

c You should _____ _____ it.

d You should _____ it.

5 **Cilka is looking in the first aid box. Scan the page of the manual and write the names for these things.**

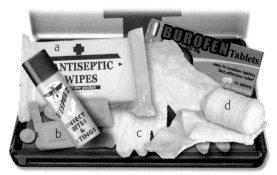

a ___antiseptic wipes___ _____

b _____

c _____

d _____

Learning tip

When you read instructions, you need to identify the most important information in each sentence – this tells you what you have to do. Writers often use commas (,) to separate a word or a group of words from another word / group of words in the sentence. You can use commas to help you work out which is the most important part of the sentence.

6 **Read the instructions under the second heading. Decide which is the most important part of each sentence. Tick ✓ the correct option.**

a 1 Using a fresh swab or wipe for each stroke, ☐

  2 clean around the wound, ☐

  3 working from the edge of the wound outwards. ☐

b 1 Carefully pick off any loose foreign matter, ☐

  2 such as glass, metal, or gravel, ☐

  3 from or around the wound.

7 **Read the instructions under the third heading. Underline the most important part of the sentence.**

8 **Read the instructions under the fourth heading. Which is the most important part of the first two sentences? When should you do these things? Complete the chart.**

	You should	when the cut/graze is
a		
b		

9 **Read all the instructions under the fourth heading again. What else should you do? Make notes.**

_____

_____

_____

_____

_____

Focus on ...

stop

1 Complete these sentences from the text

  a Small cuts and grazes soon stop _____ treatment.

  b Your aims Stop _____ _____ infected.

2 Underline the correct words in this sentence:

  In sentence a above, 'stop' means *finish / prevent* and in sentence b, 'stop' means *finish / prevent*.

3 Match the beginnings and endings of these sentences. Then decide if the verb means *finish* (F) or *prevent* (P).

  a It's not funny –

  b Health workers are trying to

  c When Cilka gave the boy a sweet, he

  d If you want to have more free time,

  e The girl was a good swimmer and she

  f My dad looked very serious, and that

  1 stopped me from laughing. ____

  2 stop watching so much TV. ____

  3 please stop laughing. __F__

  4 stop the disease from spreading. ____

  5 stopped crying. ____

  6 stopped the child from drowning. ____

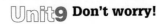

B Going to A&E

1 Cilka and her friend Marta were playing squash when Cilka fell and cut her head. They have gone to A&E in a taxi. A nurse has looked at Cilka's injury and told her to wait. Cilka is reading this leaflet while she is waiting for treatment. Skim the leaflet and match topics a–d with the paragraphs.

a what might happen after your visit to A&E ☐
b how staff decide if you are able to wait for treatment ☐
c conditions that don't need A&E treatment ☐
d why people may have to wait ☐

How do Accident and Emergency departments work?

¹ When you reach the A&E department, you will be assessed straightaway by a qualified person (this could be a nurse or a doctor). You might be treated immediately, but more often you will have to wait for treatment. How quickly you are treated will usually depend on:

- How serious your injury or condition is
- How busy the department is, and
- Whether your condition will get worse if left

The process is the same even if you arrive at the A&E department by ambulance.

² Depending on your injuries, you may be treated by a nurse or a doctor. Often, you will be allowed to go home after your treatment. If your injuries or condition is more serious, then you might be sent for an X-ray or admitted to hospital for further treatment. When you are allowed to go home, you will normally have to make your own arrangements to get home from the hospital.

³ **Waiting in A&E units**

Sometimes, you may have to wait, even though your injury seems quite serious and you are in pain (e.g. broken bones, dislocations, serious cuts). This can happen if the department is busy treating people with even more serious injuries, for example after a serious road traffic accident or after disasters such as train crashes or terrorist attacks. Waiting can be frustrating, but please bear in mind that hospital staff do all they can to treat people as quickly as possible.

⁴ If you do not need immediate care, then you may be referred to another part of the NHS. For instance, you may be advised to make an appointment to see your GP or told to call NHS Direct for advice. This often happens if your injury is minor or if your accident happened more than 24 hours before going to the department.

Did you know ...?

A&E stands for 'Accident and Emergency'.
GP stands for 'General Practitioner' (a doctor who sees people in the local area and treats illnesses which do not need a hospital visit).
NHS stands for 'National Health Service'. NHS Direct is a telephone helpline that you can call for advice.

Class bonus

Work in pairs. Another friend of Cilka's (you choose the name) wants to know what happened. The friend wants to know how the accident happened, how Cilka got to hospital, how long she waited and what treatment she had. Make a list of questions. (The text will give you ideas for some of your questions.)

Then work with a different partner. One of you is Cilka and the other is the friend. Act out the conversation.

E X tra practice

What do you think Cilka should do when she gets home? Look up *head injury* on the NHS website www.nhsdirect.nhs.uk and find out what advice it gives. What advice would you give Cilka? Make notes.

2 Do you think Cilka's injury is very serious? Read the leaflet again and find reasons for your answer. Write one or two sentences.

   I think / I don't think Cilka's injury is very serious because ....
   ....
   ....

3 Read the first paragraph again. What are the two most important points in this paragraph? Complete these sentences.

   a *You* ....
   b *You* ....

4 Skim the other paragraphs. <u>Underline</u> the most important points in each paragraph.

5 Read the text again. What are the main differences in A&E treatment for someone with a minor injury and someone with a serious injury? Write four sentences for each.

Minor injury	Serious injury
Someone with a minor injury may have to wait.	

6 After waiting four hours, Cilka's head cut was treated. How would she then go home?

Can-do checklist

Tick what you can do.

	Can do	Need more practice
I can identify the most important parts of sentences.	✔	✔
I can follow instructions in a first aid manual and give first aid.		✔
I can find out about treatment at Accident and Emergency (A&E).		

Unit 10
What's in the news?

Get ready to read

○ Read this headline from a newspaper article.

MAN FINDS CAR AFTER SEVEN MONTHS

There are five sentences in the article. Here are the beginnings of each sentence. How do you think the sentences continue?

a Motorist Eric King has been reunited with his car – …

b Eric, 57, left his black Ford Focus in a space in Bury St Edmunds, Suffolk, last February, …

c But when he had finished his sightseeing trip, …

d He returned to Bury St Edmunds ten times to look for his car, …

e He finally got the car back this week …

○ Here are the endings of each sentence. Match the parts. Write the letters in the boxes.

1 after it was reported abandoned where he had left it. $\boxed{e}$

2 he couldn't remember the name of the residential road he had parked in. $\boxed{}$

3 often booking himself into bed and breakfasts. $\boxed{}$

4 seven months after forgetting where he had parked it. $\boxed{}$

5 so that he could walk into the town centre. $\boxed{}$

○ Have you ever read an unusual – or funny – story in the newspaper? What were main points of the story?

go to Useful language p. 85

A What's it about?

1 You are going to read three short articles. These are their headlines. Use your dictionary if necessary and answer the questions.

a What do you think has happened in each article?

b Are these unusual stories?

1 **Ball boy scores goal**

2 **Father breaks leg 'curing' daughter's fear of heights**

3 **'Ugly' goldfish gets cosmetic surgery**

2 Look at the words below. Match five of the words with each article. Write numbers 1, 2 or 3 in the boxes. Do not check your answers at this stage.

bottom ☐   bridge ☐   cyst ☐
eye ☐   goalkeeper ☐   hurt ☐
jump ☐   knife ☐   nervous ☐
net ☐   operation ☐   pitch ☐
pond ☐   referee ☐   wide ☐

3 What do you think might happen in each article? Write a sentence about each one with some of the words from Exercise 2.

4 Read the three articles on the opposite page. Check your answers to Exercise 2.

5 Compare your sentences in Exercise 3 with the three articles. Which of your guesses were correct?

6 Five of the words in Exercise 2 are connected with football. Read the article about football again. Underline any other words that are connected with football.

1

Ball boy scores goal

A Brazilian referee faces suspension after she awarded a goal that was scored by a ball boy.

The 89th minute goal allowed Santacruzense to snatch a 1–1 draw at home to Atletico Sorocaba on Sunday in the Paulista Football Federation Cup, a regional tournament played in the state of Sao Paulo.

Television pictures showed that after a Santacruzense player shot narrowly wide, the boy collected the ball with his feet and took it back on to the pitch. However, instead of returning it to the goalkeeper, he subtly tapped it across the line into the net.

Although there were nearly ten seconds between the shot going out and the boy placing the ball over the line, referee Silvia Regina da Oliveira awarded a goal amid furious Sorocaba protests.

2

Father breaks leg 'curing' daughter's fear of heights

A man and his 10-year-old daughter were on an evening bike ride when he suggested they jump off the Lantana Bridge and into the Intracoastal Waterway.

The nervous little girl agreed and at 7.40pm on Monday, Troy Stewart, 31, grabbed his daughter's hand, counted to three and jumped nearly 20 feet into the water. Megan Stewart was not hurt, but her father broke his left leg when he hit the bottom.

"He thought he could break her fear of heights by doing that. Instead, he broke his leg" said Lantana Police Captain Andy Rundle. "I wouldn't consider this an appropriate method of trying to break your kid of a phobia. She could have got hurt too."

They had to swim about 50 feet to shore, and Megan ran two blocks home to get her mother, Mandy Potter.

3

'Ugly' goldfish gets cosmetic surgery

A goldfish on show at a museum has undergone cosmetic surgery after visitors at the museum said it looked ugly.

The fish, which lives in a pond at the Royal Museum of Scotland in Edinburgh, went under the knife to remove an unsightly cyst from its eye.

Although the growth was harmless, some visitors had expressed concern about the creature's appearance and it was removed as a precaution, along with one of its eyes.

The operation was paid for using coins thrown into the fishpond at the museum.

Focus on …
verbs in headlines

1 Complete the headlines of the three articles.
   a Ball boy .... goal
   b Father .... leg 'curing' daughter's fear of heights
   c 'Ugly' goldfish .... cosmetic surgery

2 In which tense are the verbs in the headlines above? Underline the correct tense.
   a present perfect
   b present simple
   c past simple

3 Now read the first two articles and find another form of the same verb. Which tense are the verbs? Complete the chart for articles 1 and 2.

Article	Verb in article	Tense
1		
2		
3		

4 Now read the third article. Find a different verb which means the same as the verb in the headline. Which tense is the verb? Complete the chart for article 3.

5 Look at these newspaper headlines. Write the first sentence of each article.
   a Police rescue UK tourist from Outback twice in one week
   b Wife kills pet spiders in toilet
   c New child seat laws come into force
   d Shoppers leave OAP trapped in a hole

7 **Read the articles again. Write six questions for each article beginning with these words:** *who, what, when, where, why, how.* **Make sure that the answers to your questions are in the articles.**

Class bonus

Exchange your questions with another student. Can you answer your partner's questions?

8 **Which of these stories do you think is the most unusual – or funny?**

B Strange, but true!

1 Think about your answers to these questions. Check that you know the meaning of the words in *italics*.

a Have you got a *bank account*?
b Where is the nearest *branch* of your bank?
c How do you pay for things you buy?
d How often do you get a *bank statement*?
e Have you ever been in *debt*?

2 Look quickly at the text below. Where does it come from?

3 Look at the headline. Use the dictionary entries on the right for help if necessary. Answer these questions.

a What do you think has happened?
b Why is this unusual?

---

ban¹ /bæn/ *verb* [T] **banning** *past* **banned** to officially say that someone must not do something *A lot of people think boxing should be banned.* ◦ [+ **from** + **doing** sth] *Ian's been banned from driving for 2 years.*

---

vicar /ˈvɪkər/ *noun* [C] a priest in some Christian churches

---

overdrawn /ˌəʊvəˈdrɔːn/ *adjective* If you are overdrawn, you have taken more money out of your bank account than you had in it. *We've gone £200 overdrawn!*

---

4 Look at the photograph. Who can you see? Scan the article and circle the person's name.

5 Scan the article again. <u>Underline</u> the names of any other people and places.

Bank bans vicar's son for life for going 11p overdrawn

by **Geoff Maynard**

Bank chiefs have banned a schoolboy for life because his account went 11 pence into the red.

Vicar's son Jerome Jacob, 15, was told he could never have another account at HSBC, despite offering to repay the money.

Jerome, who holds down two part-time jobs in between studying for his GCSEs, went overdrawn when he bought a football magazine using his debit card.

After receiving a monthly statement, Jerome and his father, the Reverend Neville Jacob, went into their local branch in Romsey, Hampshire, to clear the debt. But they were amazed when staff told them the account had been closed and they could not open a new one.

Jerome said: "Their customer service was awful. When I opened the account, they told me it would be impossible to go overdrawn when using my card."

Mr Jacob, vicar of Copthorne, Hampshire, added: "We don't fault the bank for applying its rules. All we wanted was a bit of common sense."

"My son was willing to repay the 11p and apologise, but they just were not interested. It was a flat refusal. My son was quite upset."

"It's the first time he has gone overdrawn and I'm astonished at their attitude. To say he can never go back is ridiculous and the way he was treated was outrageous. If they treated adults this way, they would soon be out of business."

A spokesman for HSBC said: "This does not appear to be in line with our commitment to our customers. Being overdrawn by 11p would not trigger the decision to close the account and we will be investigating this incident."

Jerome, who does a paper round and works part-time in a tea room, has now applied for a Barclays account.

Did you know …?

In the UK, there are two types of newspapers. Tabloids are traditionally small newspapers with a lot of pictures and short, simple news stories (e.g. *Daily Express, The Sun, Daily Mirror*). *The Times, The Daily Telegraph, The Guardian, The Independent,* etc. are more serious newspapers and more difficult to read. These newspapers used to be large and they were called broadsheets. Now all newspapers are more or less the same size. The article on the opposite page is from the *Daily Express*.

6 **In which order did Jerome do these things?**

a   He got his monthly bank statement. ☐

b   He went to the bank with his dad. ☐

c   He opened a bank account at HSBC. ☐1☐

d   He found out he was overdrawn. ☐

e   He decided to open an account with another bank. ☐

f   He used his debit card to buy a magazine. ☐

g   He said he would pay the money he owed. ☐

7 **What did bank staff do? Write a list of sentences. Number your sentences in the correct order in which they happened.**

1   The bank staff allowed Jerome to open an account.

----

8 **What does Jerome's father think about the situation? Which adjectives does he use to express his opinion? Complete the sentences.**

Jerome's father is .... at the attitude of the bank. He thinks it is .... (of the bank) to say that Jerome cannot go back (and open another account), and the way he was treated is ....

Learning tip

Reading for pleasure is the best way to improve your reading. It is also a wonderful way to meet new words. Identify words that are useful to you and keep a vocabulary notebook of these words. Give each page a title, e.g. *sport, education*, and write useful words in a list. For each word, note the meaning, the part of speech (noun, verb, etc.), anything special about its grammar or style (formal, informal, etc.) and write a sentence which is relevant to you.

9 <u>Underline</u> **the words in** *italics* **in Exercise 1 in the text.** <u>Underline</u> **other words in the text which are connected with banking. Add the words to your vocabulary notebook. If you do not have a vocabulary notebook start one now!**

E✗tra practice

Read an article in an English-language newspaper or look on the Internet. Perhaps find something you have read about in your own language. Ask yourself and answer questions beginning with *who, what, when, where, why* and *how* about the article.

Can-do checklist

Tick what you can do.

	Can do	Need more practice
I can use headlines to predict the content of newspaper articles.	✔	✔
I can understand short newspaper articles.		
I can identify words that are useful to me.		

Unit 11
I'll check my email

Get ready to read

- Who do you get emails from? Tick ✓ your answers.

my friends ☐	e-pals around the world ☐
my family ☐	my dentist ☐
my colleagues at work ☐	travel companies ☐
other students of English ☐	shops and stores ☐

- Who do you send emails to? Write a list.

  ....

  ....

  ....

go to Useful language p. 85

A It's from a friend

Learning tip

When you read a message that someone has sent you, always ask yourself why the person has sent you the message. Think about its main purpose before you read more carefully for the details. This will help you to understand the message more easily.

1 Read the three emails and match each one with its main purpose.

email 1	makes a request
email 2	makes a suggestion
email 3	gives a warning

Did you know ...?

giuliamartinuzzo@yahoo.com is Giulia's email address. We say this as: Giulia Martinuzzo at Yahoo dot com.

1

To:	Giulia Martinuzzo
From:	Ryuichi Tashita
Subject:	Pizza

Sorry I missed your call yesterday. Yeah, the new pizzeria sounds great. I'm not here all next week, but the following Friday's fine. Why not see if Raquel's free as well? TAFN

2 New Message

File   Edit   View   Insert   Format   Tools   Message   Help

To:	giuliamartinuzzo@yahoo.com
From:	Sara Loefler
Subject:	Your arrival

What time does your train get to Brighton on Friday? Can't meet you at the station if it's in the morning 'cos I've got an exam. ☹

3

To:	Giulia M
From:	Ewa
Subject:	Photos

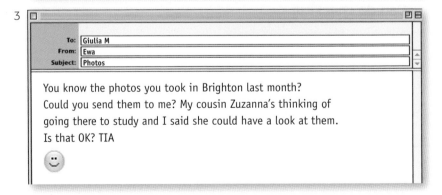

You know the photos you took in Brighton last month?
Could you send them to me? My cousin Zuzanna's thinking of going there to study and I said she could have a look at them. Is that OK? TIA

☺

Focus on ...
email English

ab**C**def

The English used in emails is usually informal because people often write in the way they speak. They use short forms of words and miss out some words. They also use abbreviations, such as BTW (by the way) and IMO (in my opinion). They also use 'smileys', such as ☺ (I'm happy).

Circle two abbreviations and a 'smiley' in the emails on the opposite page. What do you think they mean? Here are some clues:

T = *thanks* or *that's*
A = *all* or *advance*

Work out abbreviations for these expressions.

a as far as I know ....
b for your information ....
c hope that helps ....
d in other words ....

2 Read the emails on the opposite page again. Then decide which sentences are correct. Circle A, B or C.

1 A Ryuichi is unavailable for a meal next week.
  B Raquel can join Giulia for a meal next Friday.
  C Giulia doesn't want to have a pizza.
2 A Sara will be able to see Giulia early Friday morning.
  B Giulia needs to arrive in time for Sara's exam on Friday.
  C Sara can collect Giulia from the station on Friday afternoon.
3 A Ewa wants to study in Brighton.
  B Zuzanna would like to find out about Brighton.
  C Giulia's thinking of taking some photographs of Ewa.

3 Read the emails on the right and choose the best answer for each question. Circle A, B or C.

1 Why has Stefan emailed Giulia?
  A to give her some details
  B to let her know that he's ill
  C to remind her to do something

2 Why has Raquel emailed Giulia?
  A to thank her for lunch
  B to offer her congratulations
  C to give her some information

4 Read all the emails again. What do you find out about Giulia? Write six sentences.

Her _family name is Martinuzzo._
She ....
Her ....
She ....
She ....
She ....

5 Read this reply to one of the emails. Which of her five friends is Giulia emailing?

I'm working every day this week, so won't leave before 6pm. Will get a taxi to your flat. Good luck BTW!
Giulia X

6 Choose one of the other emails. Imagine you are Giulia and write a reply.

Class bonus

Exchange email addresses with another student in your class and become e-pals. Try and write to each other in English every week.

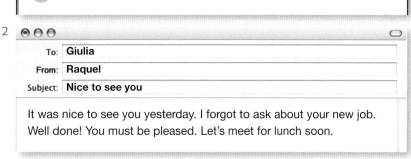

1 New Message
File Edit View Insert Format Tools Message Help
To: Giulia Martinuzzo
From: Stefan Amundsen
Subject: Film club

Feeling any better? Don't forget to register for the film club. Email me if you want any information about it. BTW the first film is *The Importance of Being Ernest*. IMO it's great!

☺

2
To: Giulia
From: Raquel
Subject: Nice to see you

It was nice to see you yesterday. I forgot to ask about your new job. Well done! You must be pleased. Let's meet for lunch soon.

B What's your address?

1 Look at the six emails in Giulia's inbox. Complete the chart with the answers to these questions.

a Who are the emails from?

b Which ones are replies to emails that Giulia sent?

c What is the main purpose of each email?

	Who from?	Reply?	Main purpose?
1	Sally Jones	no	give her new email address
2			
3			
4			
5			
6			

1

Dear all
Please note that my new email address is

sallyljones@btinternet.com
love
Sally

2

Dear Giulia
This is just a test to see if I've got your right address.
Hope you're well!
Love Yvonne

3

File Edit View Insert Format Tools Message Help

Hi. This is the qmail-send program at yahoo.com.
I'm afraid I wasn't able to deliver your message to the following addresses.
This is a permanent error; I've given up. Sorry it didn't work out.

<saraloefler@virgin.net>:
64.97.139.1 does not like recipient.
Remote host said: 550 RCPT TO:< saraloefler@virgin.net>
User unknown
Giving up on 64.97.139.1.

--------- Below this line is a copy of the message. ---------

I'm working every day this week, so won't leave before 6pm. Will get a taxi to your flat. Good luck BTW!
Giulia X

4

Hello. I am away until 10 October and am unable to read my email until I return.
Ryuichi

5

Hi Giulia,
6 of my friends have joined my network so far on PALSINC. Join me and my friends on PALSINC and meet more than 6 MILLION members from all around the world!

Join Marcos's Network

Learn more
Name: Marcos Martos Higueras
Current Location: Barcelona, Catalunya, Spain
Home Location: Barcelona, Catalunya, Spain
Gender: Male
Age: 31

This invitation was sent to giuliamartinuzzo@yahoo.com on behalf of Marcos (mmh@hotmail.com).

If you do not wish to receive invitations from Marcos, click here.

If you do not wish to receive invitations from any member, click here.

6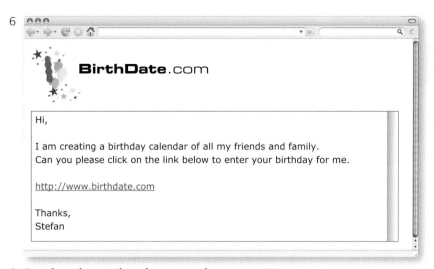

2 Read each email and answer these questions.

a Which email do you think Giulia should reply to?

----

b What should she do when she receives the others?

----

3 Giulia would like to receive a birthday card from Stefan. She has already clicked on the link. What should she do next?

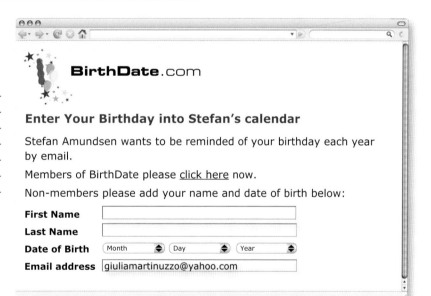

4 Enter your own birthday into Stefan's calendar.

5 Do you ever receive any emails like the ones on these pages? Who are they from?

E✗tra practice

There are lots of sites on the Internet which can reunite you with old friends – one of these is called 'WAYN'. WAYN stands for 'Where are you now?' Read more about this website on www.wayn.com. If you want to, you can join.

Can-do checklist

Tick what you can do.

	Can do	Need more practice
I can work out the main purpose of an email.		
I can understand email abbreviations and 'smileys'.	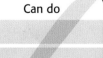	
I can identify different types of email and deal with them.		

Review 1
Units 1–11

A Are these statements true (T) or false (F)?

1 If you are looking for a particular piece of information, you'll need to read every word of a text in order to find it. .... (Unit 1)

2 If you want to get a general idea of what a text is about, you must read from the beginning and continue to the end. .... (Unit 2)

3 It is not necessary to understand every word in a text you are reading. .... (Unit 3)

4 As you read a text, try and work out the meaning of any words you do not know. .... (Unit 4)

5 There is no point in trying to work out the function of each sentence – this would not help you at all. .... (Unit 5)

6 Thinking about a topic in your own language can help you to understand a text about the topic. .... (Unit 6)

7 When you come across an unknown word in a text, look out for words which might have the same or a similar meaning. .... (Unit 7)

8 When you want to compare two or more things that are mentioned in a text, using a chart is a good way to take notes. .... (Unit 8)

9 Writers only use commas to separate words in lists. .... (Unit 9)

10 You can learn a lot of useful words through reading. .... (Unit 10)

11 Some emails you receive do not have a real purpose. .... (Unit 11)

B Now read the *Learning tips* for Units 1–11 on pages 87–89. Do you want to change any of your answers in Exercise A?

C The first time we read a text, we usually either skim or scan it. Can you remember the difference between skimming and scanning? Complete these definitions.

12 If you .... a text, you know exactly what you are looking for and you search through the text quickly until you find that specific piece of information.

13 If you .... a text, you want to get a general idea and you look at the text quickly without focusing on any details.

D Look at this list of real-life reading situations. Circle the text type in each situation. Then decide whether you would skim or scan the text in each situation. Tick ✓ the correct box.

14 You are in London. You are looking at a notice about opening hours outside a bank. You want to know if banks in Britain are open the same hours in your country.
scan ☐ skim ☐

15 You are looking at a theatre programme. You want to know what is on in the last week of the month.
scan ☐ skim ☐

16 You are reading a restaurant review. You want to know where the restaurant is.
scan ☐ skim ☐

17 You are looking at a leaflet about a tourist attraction. You are trying to decide whether to go there or not.
scan ☐ skim ☐

18 You are looking at a page in a newspaper. You are trying to find an article that interests you.
scan ☐ skim ☐

19 You have just received an email from your friend Luis. You want to find out if he passed his exam.
scan ☐ skim ☐

E The way we read a text depends on our purpose in reading. Two people can read the same text in a different way. Think about the text types in Exercise D again. Complete the sentences with *scan* or *skim* and the text types.

20 You would .... to find out if the writer liked the restaurant.

21 You would .... to find out if the bank is open on Saturday morning.

22 You would .... to find out what kind of shows are on this month.

23 You would .... to find out how much it costs to go in.

24 You would .... to find out if it is just for you or for lots of people.

25 You would .... to find out if your football team won yesterday.

F Skim these texts. What is each text, or where does it come from? Choose from the following.

a cinema programme	an email
a hospital notice	a hostel leaflet
a phone box notice	a post office leaflet
a guidebook	a newspaper article
a theatre programme	

26 Text A   ------------------------------

27 Text B   ------------------------------

G Read Text A again. Which five sentences describe Slava's Snowshow? Write the letters in the boxes.

28–32

☐ ☐ ☐ ☐ ☐

a The director is from New York.
b Slava's Snowshow has been on tour.
c Scarlett Johansson loves the show.
d Slava's Snowshow is a musical.
e There is more than one performer in Slava's Snowshow.
f It is freezing cold in the theatre during a performance.
g Children enjoy Slava's Snowshow.
h You can buy a book about Slava's Snowshow.
i Tickets for the show are on sale now.
j The show is on during the second week in March.

Text A

DIRECT FROM NEW YORK

Slava's SNOWSHOW

Created and staged by Slava

A global phenomenon, Slava's Snowshow has entertained audiences in over 80 cities around the world with fans including Angelina Jolie and Scarlett Johansson.

Slava's Snowshow is an unmissable comedy masterpiece. Slava and his ensemble of clowns use water, cobwebs, bubbles and dry ice with dazzling effect. The show ends with a snowstorm in which the audience is engulfed in a blizzard of sparkling snowflakes.

Slava's Snowshow is full of laughter and enjoyment for the whole family. Book now for the snow sensation of the season.

Mon 21 March – Sat 28 March

H Decide if these sentences about Text B are true (T) or false (F).

33 You can always have lunch at a taverna. ......
34 Tavernas do not always have a menu to choose from. ......
35 The baked dishes are usually cakes or desserts. ......
36 The main course usually arrives after the starter. ......
37 Vegetable dishes like stuffed peppers are quite big. ......

Text B

Travel: Greece

The best place to eat and drink in Greece is the taverna. These stay open late in the evening and some tavernas are open at lunchtime too. You won't always find a menu in a taverna –and when there is one, it is never very long. Usually, there will be five or six *mezédes* (starters or snacks) and three of four main courses. Often you are taken into the kitchen to inspect what's on offer that day: uncooked meat – usually lamb – and fish, pans of stew and vegetables, trays of baked savoury dishes.

Starters and main courses are usually served together in Greece. If you prefer to have the two courses separately, then order your main course when your starter arrives. Main courses of meat or fish do not include salads and vegetables – you will need to order these as side dishes. You may not want to eat meat or fish as many of the vegetable dishes are delicious. You could quite easily have tomatoes, peppers or aubergines stuffed with rice as a main course.

I Skim these texts. What is each text, or where does it come from? Choose from the following.

a cinema programme	an email
a hospital notice	a hostel leaflet
a phone box notice	a post office leaflet
a guidebook	a newspaper article
a theatre programme	

38 Text C _____
39 Text D _____
40 Text E _____

Text C

yha Accommodation prices at YHA Manchester

Adults £20.50

Under 18s £15.50

This is for a bed in a shared room – max 6 persons

Family/Private rooms – calculated on no. of adults & no. of under 18s

Twin room £52.00

All rooms are en-suite and all prices are per night and include a full breakfast and bed linen

YHA members receive a £3 discount per member per night

Group prices and conference rates available on request

Text D

Women trapped in car

Two elderly women are recovering from heat stroke and heat exhaustion after locking themselves in a hot car in Daytona Beach, Florida.

Police say that their battery apparently died, the automatic locks failed, and they didn't know they could unlock the doors manually.

The women were trapped for nearly two hours before a passerby spotted their pleas for help, which they wrote on the back of a tissue box.

Rescue workers smashed a window to get the ladies out.

Text E

Who are you?

To make sure that you receive the safest possible care whilst being treated, it is important that we identify you correctly at all times.

Therefore, before you have any test, treatment or procedure, before you see a doctor or nurse in outpatients, and before you are given any medication, we will ask you to identify yourself.

We will ask you to state:
● your full name or hospital number (if you have one)
● your date of birth

Sometimes we may ask for other details, such as your address.
If you look after a child, or if someone you care for cannot give us this information, we may ask you to identify them on their behalf.

Although it can be annoying to be asked the same question many times, please help us to help you by making sure these important checks take place.

J Answer these questions about Text C. Write one or two words only.

41 How many beds are there in a shared room? _____
42 Can I have a room of my own? _____
43 Are twin rooms cheaper per person than shared rooms? _____
44 Is breakfast included in the price? _____
45 How much cheaper is it if I am a member of the YHA? _____

K Read Text D again. In which order did these things happen? Write the letters in the boxes. There is one extra sentence which is not part of the story.

46 ☐   47 ☐   48 ☐   49 ☐   50 ☐

a Someone saw a message the women had written.
b The women were rescued from the car.
c The women broke the car window.
d The women didn't know how to get out of the car.
e The car battery stopped working.
f The rescue services were called.

L Read Text E again. Underline the correct word or phrase in these sentences.

51 You *can receive / can't receive* treatment before staff know who you are.
52 You *may not have / must have* a hospital number.
53 You *don't have to give / must give* your date of birth.
54 You *might have to identify / won't have to identify* yourself more than once.
55 You *may have to say / will have to say* your address.

M Where would you see these notices? Match the notices with the places. Write the letters in the boxes.

56 bank ☐
57 optician's ☐
58 theatre ☐
59 airport ☐
60 book shop ☐
61 A&E ☐
62 post box ☐
63 restaurant ☐
64 cable car ☐
65 bus stop ☐

N Look at the notices again. Tick ✓ the correct explanation.

66 A 1 The driver sells tickets. ☐
   2 You can't buy a ticket from the driver. ☐
67 B 1 You might get hurt. ☐
   2 The window should be closed at all times. ☐
68 C 1 We sell books for students. ☐
   2 We will sell your old books. ☐
69 D 1 You can't post your letters and postcards after 7.00pm. ☐
   2 You can post your letters and postcards for abroad here. ☐
70 E 1 There is only one cashier working here. ☐
   2 You may have to wait to be seen. ☐
71 F 1 You must carry your bags with you at all times. ☐
   2 Your luggage should be checked in. ☐
72 G 1 The show has one interval only. ☐
   2 If you are late, you will miss the first part of the show. ☐
73 H 1 Not everything will be half price. ☐
   2 All designer brands will be half price. ☐
74 I 1 Only people from this country get free treatment. ☐
   2 Some people have to pay for their treatment. ☐
75 J 1 You can choose an expensive dish and still only pay £5. ☐
   2 You can eat a lot if you want to. ☐

A

Latecomers will not be admitted until the first interval.

B

Are you an **OVERSEAS VISITOR?**
Did you know that you may have to pay for hospital treatment whilst here?

C

HALF PRICE SALE
Up to 50% OFF
Selected frames and sunglasses including designer brands.

D

New books for the new term
With an excellent range of titles and knowledgeable sfaff, we can cater for all your book-buying needs

E

BUY YOUR TICKET HERE
BEFORE BOARDING

F

FIRST CLASS AND INTERNATIONAL MAIL
Last collection time 7.00 pm

G

DO NOT LEAVE
LUGGAGE OR OTHER
BELONGINGS
UNATTENDED

H

HELP YOURSELF
BUFFET
ALL YOU CAN EAT
FOR £5!

I

DO NOT LEAN OUT
OF THE WINDOW

J

Please wait
behind the line
until a cashier
is available

O You are in Denmark, and you have picked up the brochure *Copenhagen This Week*. Answer these questions.

76 Skim the text. What is the main aim of the article? Choose from these options.
  a to explain why the gardens have been closed ☐
  b to give tourists a general introduction ☐
  c to describe the gardens and flowers ☐

77 Which of these topics does the article NOT mention? Circle the correct letter.
  a the opening hours
  b the history of the gardens
  c other tourist attractions in Denmark
  d admission prices
  e the number of people who go there

Tivoli Gardens
Main entrance on Vesterbrogade 3
(map: 4/C4)

Summer Season
April 12 – September 24

Opening hours
Sunday –Thursday 11am – 11pm
Friday 11am – 0:30 am
Saturday 11am – midnight

Admission prices
Adults DKK 75, children
(aged 3–13 yrs) DKK 35

Season passes
DKK 195 (adults), DKK 110 (children)

Multi-ride tickets
DKK 200 (adults), DKK 150 (children)

Tivoli Gardens
Reopen

Tivoli Gardens – probably Europe's most sophisticated amusement park – opens on April 12 for its summer season, the event of the month! Founded in 1843 Tivoli Gardens has been in the amusement business for 163 years and draws around four million visitors a year making it Denmark's number one tourist attraction – and one of Europe's most popular amusement parks after EuroDisney Paris and Blackpool Pleasure Beach.

Sporting 25 amusements including no fewer than four big dippers and a new carousel, Tivoli is an elegant funfair in the very heart of Copenhagen, with good music in abundance throughout the season, some 40 top class eateries and restaurants, flowers and romance in the air.

World's tallest carousel

Brand new at Tivoli this season is the Austrian-built Star Flyer – the tallest carousel in the world, standing 80 metres high. This ride has a capacity of 960 passengers an hour and a maximum rotary speed of 70 kph. Star Flyer, with its galactic design and 16th century Danish astronomer Tycho Brahe's universe as its theme, is located in Tivoli's Merry Corner between the Concert Hall and the Spinning Top amusement.

Amusements account for more than 50 percent of Tivoli's turnover, helping fund the delights of the gardens such as the flowers, the music, and the firework displays.

P Find other words in the text which have similar meanings to these words.

78 sophisticated ....

79 amusement park ....

80 amusement ....

Q Find words in the text for two types of amusement.

81 ....

82 ....

R Find the names of two of the amusements at Tivoli Gardens.

83 ....

84 ....

S What is really special about the brand new amusement? Write one letter in the box.

85 ☐

a It is 80 metres high.

b It can carry 960 passengers each hour.

c It turns at a speed of 70 kilometres per hour.

d It has a galactic design.

T You have bought your admission ticket and you have gone into Tivoli Gardens. Make a list of five things you can do. Do you have to pay extra to do these things?

You can …	extra payment? Y (yes) or N (no)
86	
87	
88	
89	
90	

U Here is another part of the brochure *Copenhagen This Week*. Are these sentences about Tivoli Concert Hall true (T) or false (F)?

91 It is the biggest concert hall in Denmark. ☐

92 It was not open last summer. ☐

93 It has a new café and bar. ☐

94 It is a venue for pop and rock concerts. ☐

95 It is not open at the weekend. ☐

Tivoli Concert Season takes off

Tivoli Concert Hall – home of the biggest music festival in the Nordic region and one of Denmark's main concert venues – is back in full operation this season after being closed all last summer to undergo major refurbishment involving the construction of a new circular glass foyer with café and two-storey bar with stunning views over the gardens.

Tivoli Concert Hall's extensive summer programme involves 105 arrangements, including 20 performances by the Tivoli Symphony Orchestra and the appearance of some of the world's greatest soloists in the world of classical music. Kicking off the season at 7.30pm on April 12 is the Belcea Quartet with a Haydn, Britten and Mozart chamber concert.

Tivoli Ticket Center Tel 33 15 10 12
Vesterbrogade 3
Open: Mon–Fri 9am–5pm

V It is Saturday April 8th and you have just arrived in Copenhagen for a week's holiday. You look at the brochure and find that there's a concert you can go to. Answer these questions. Write notes.

96 What date is the concert?

....

97 What time is the concert?

....

98 Who is giving the performance?

....

99 What music are they playing?

....

100 When is the box office next open?

....

Unit 12
Is that spelt correctly?

Get ready to read

- There are some differences between British and American English. In which ways are there differences? Tick ✓ one or more of the boxes.
  - a grammar ☐
  - b pronunciation ☐
  - c spelling ☐
  - d vocabulary ☐

  Can you think of any examples?

- How good are you at spelling? Tick ✓ one of the boxes in each column.

In my own language, I'm	In English, I'm
not very good ☐ quite good ☐ very good ☐	not very good ☐ quite good ☐ very good ☐

- How do you check your spelling? Tick ✓ one or more of the boxes.
  I look in a dictionary. ☐
  I look in a book about spelling. ☐
  I use an electronic spellchecker. ☐
  I use the spellchecker on the computer. ☐
  I look at my own vocabulary word lists. ☐
  I think about where I have seen the word and look for it there. ☐

go to Useful language p. 85

A British and American English

1 Look at these words. Do you think they are British English (BE) or American English (AE) spellings?
   - a defence _BE_
   - b non-member _____
   - c traveller _____
   - d colour _____
   - e litre _____

2 The text on the opposite page is from a book called *Improve your spelling*. Scan the text and check your answers to Exercise 1. Then write the other spelling of each word.
   - a def_ense_
   - b non_____
   - c trav_____
   - d col_____
   - e lit_____

3 Scan the text again. Are these words used in British English (BE) or American English (AE) – or both? Tick ✓ the boxes.

		BE	AE	both
a	license	☐	☐	✓
b	practise	☐	☐	☐
c	chilli	☐	☐	☐
d	woollen	☐	☐	☐
e	enrol	☐	☐	☐
f	fulfilled	☐	☐	☐
g	behaviour	☐	☐	☐
h	glamour	☐	☐	☐

4 Were these questions written by British (B) or American (A) people? Tick ✓ the boxes.

		B	A
a	What flavor ice-cream do you prefer?	☐	✓
b	Are you a non-smoker?	☐	☐
c	Have you got a driving licence?	☐	☐
d	When did you last go to the theater?	☐	☐

5 Is the text about general spelling rules or individual words?

British and American English

We have really everything in common with America nowadays, except, of course, language.

Oscar Wilde

There are many differences between British and American English spelling, both in general spelling rules and in individual words. The main differences are outlined in this chapter.

ce, se

Some words that end in *ce* in British English are spelt *se* in American English:
British English *defence, offence, pretence*
American English *defense, offense, pretense*
British English *licence* (noun), *license* (verb); *practice* (noun), *practise* (verb)
American English *license* (noun and verb); *practice* (noun and verb)

Hyphens

American English uses fewer hyphens than British English. To take just one example, in American English words formed with *non-* (= 'not') are generally written as single words (*nonmember, nonsmoker*) whereas in British English, they are normally hyphenated (*non-member, non-smoker*).

Single and double *l*

Where British English doubles a final *l* before a word-ending such as *-ed* or *-ing*, in American English the final *l* is not doubled.
British English *equalled, travelling, traveller, counsellor*
American English *equaled, traveling, traveler, counselor*
Note also British English *chilli, jeweller, jewellery, marvellous, woollen* but American English *chili* or *chilli, jeweler, jewelry, marvelous, woolen.*
On the other hand, in some words where British English has a single *l*, American English has *ll*:
British English *appal, distil, enrol, enthral, fulfil, instil* or *instill, skilful, wilful*
American English *appall, distill, enroll, enthrall, fulfill, instill, skillful, willful* or less commonly *wilful*

-our, -or

Most words that end in *-our* in British English end in *-or* in American English:
British English *behaviour, colour, favour, flavour, harbour, honour*, etc.
American English *behavior, color, favor, flavor, harbor, honor*, etc.
In American English *glamour* is the preferred spelling, but *glamor* is also correct.

re, er

Most words that end in *re* in British English end in *er* in American English:
British English *centre, fibre, litre, meagre, metre, sombre, spectre, theatre*, etc.
American English *center, fiber, liter, meager, meter, somber, specter, theater*, etc.

---

6 Look at the pictures. Match the British English words with the pictures.

axe   cheque   doughnut   grey
~~kerb~~ moustache pyjamas   tyre

a _____kerb_____   e _____
b _____   f _____
c _____   g _____
d _____   h _____

7 Write the American English spellings of the words in Exercise 6. Check in a dictionary if necessary.

a _____curb_____
b _____
c _____
d _____
e _____
f _____
g _____
h _____

Class bonus

Choose six of the words from this section of the unit – either British English or American English spelling. Make sure you can spell the words aloud. Work in pairs. Spell your words to your partner. Write down your partner's words. Then decide if they are British or American English – or can they be both?

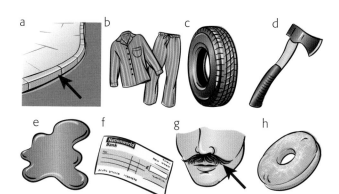

a   b   c   d

e   f   g   h

B I'll add it to my dictionary

1 Skim the extract
CORRECTING SPELLING
MISTAKES. What kind of
book is this text from?

----

2 Look at the sentence
below. Read CORRECTING
SPELLING MISTAKES again
and find out what this
shortcut is showing.

CORRECTING SPELLING MISTAKES

You might notice red wavy lines under some of your text. These lines flag
possible spelling errors because the automatic Spelling Checker is activated.
Once you are finished typing your document, you can go back and edit flagged
text. To do this, right-click the flagged word. A shortcut menu is displayed,
giving you some correctly spelled words to choose from. You can ignore the
suggestions if you like. You can also choose to add the flagged words to a
customized dictionary that you build, which can include specialized terms,
acronyms, and names that are not included in the standard Word dictionary.
If you add a word, it will no longer be underlined as a possible spelling error in
later documents.

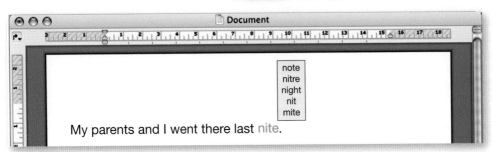

My parents and I went there last nite.

note
nitre
night
nit
mite

3 Read the extract below. How would you add the correct spelling of
nite to your customized dictionary? <u>Underline</u> the part of the text
which tells you what to do.

USING AUTOCORRECT

The AutoCorrect feature allows you to set up the automatic correction of words that you
often misspell or mistype. Many common errors are already set up in AutoCorrect, but you
can easily add you own. You can also use it to capitalize words, such as days of the week, and
to insert symbols such as © by entering (c).

1 AUTOCORRECT: ADDING WORDS
- As an example, we'll use the common misspelling: **decieve** for **deceive**.
- Click on **Tools** on the Menu bar and then on **AutoCorrect**.
- The **AutoCorrect** dialog box opens. Click on the **AutoCorrect** tab
to bring it to the front. In the **Replace:** text box enter the incorrect
spelling: **decieve**. In the **With:** text box, enter the correct spelling:
deceive. Then click on **Add**.
- The AutoCorrect entry that you have just made is now displayed in the
list of AutoCorrect entries. Click on **Close** and each time that you now
type **decieve**, it will be replaced automatically with the correct spelling

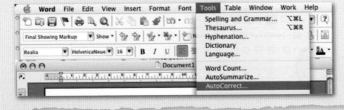

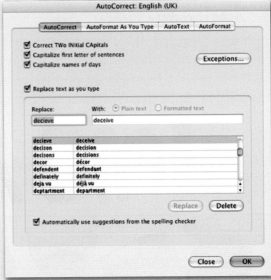

Did you know …?

US English spelling	British English spelling
spelled	spelled *or* spelt
customize	customize *or* customise
specialize	specialize *or* specialise
capitalize	capitalize *or* capitalise
dialog	dialogue *(but US spelling is always used for computers)*

Learning tip

Reading, as well as giving pleasure and information, has other advantages. It allows you to see how other people write and how they punctuate their work. You will also see a wide range of vocabulary – and how these words are spelt. Always make a note of the correct spelling of any useful words which you might need for your writing.

Focus on …
spelling

Look at the words below. Which ones are NOT spelt correctly? Read the extracts on the opposite page again and check your answers. Write the correct spelling of the words.

a displaid ___displayed___
b dictionary _____
c errer _____
d feeture _____
e mispell _____
f simbols _____
g entrys _____
h aotomatically _____

4 Which of the words in the *Focus on spelling* do you often spell incorrectly? Would you add the correct spelling to your autocorrect feature?

5 Look at this list of the top ten spelling errors often made by learners of English. Which word in each pair is spelt correctly? <u>Underline</u> the correct spelling. Do not check your answers at this stage.

a accomodation   <u>accommodation</u>
b sincerely   sincerly
c advertisment   advertisement
d wich   which
e because   becose
f beginning   begining
g comfortable   confortable
h successful   successfull
i embarassing   embarrassing
j receive   recieve

6 Check the spellings in Exercise 5. Use one of the ways you ticked in *Get ready to read*.

E X tra practice

Which words do you often make spelling mistakes with? Make a list which you can use to check your written work.

Can-do checklist

Tick what you can do.

	Can do	Need more practice
I can identify British English and American English spellings.	✔	✔
I can add words to the computer's customized dictionary.		
I can identify incorrect spellings.		

Get ready to read

○ <u>Underline</u> the words in these sentences so that they are true for you.

I read / I don't read a lot in my everyday life.

I read / I don't read magazines and newspapers.

I read / I don't read books and novels.

I buy / I don't buy books from shops or online.

There's / There isn't a library near my home/school.

I use / I don't use a library.

I borrow / I don't borrow books from the library.

I read / I don't read magazines and newspapers in the library.

○ Write two more sentences that are true for you. Use the words in brackets.

....

.... (read)

....

.... (library)

go to Useful language p. 85

A Joining a library

1 You are thinking of joining a public library in Oxford. What kind of things do you want to know about joining the library? Write down three questions.

a ....

b ....

c ....

Learning tip

When you read a difficult piece of text, you will need to read some words and sentences very carefully. In order to understand difficult parts of texts, it is a good idea to try and put the sentences of the text into your own words.

2 Some of your friends are already library members. Read what they have said about using libraries in Oxford. Then read the text from the Oxfordshire County Council website on the opposite page and decide if what your friends say is true (T) or false (F). Correct the information that is false.

a Foreign students can join the library.   ..T..

b You can get an application form online.   ......

c You can borrow ten books at a time.   ......

d You can also hire videos and DVDs.   ......

e You must return CDs after one week or pay extra.   ......

f You must take your books to the library if you want them out again.   ......

Oxfordshire County Council

Page 1 of 1

Join a library

It's free to join a library. Find out how to join and borrow books, videos and other media.

Who can join a library?

Everyone is welcome: adults and children alike are free to browse, read books, newspapers or magazines, ask for information and join in organised activities.

In order to borrow books or to hire videos or other media, you will need to join the library. Membership is free, and open to everyone living, working or studying in Oxfordshire.

Above all, library services are provided for you. No-one is too young or too old to join the library. Our staff are eager to help you get the most from your service. Just ask!

How to join

Fill in an application form (available from any Oxfordshire library) and provide confirmation of your name, address and signature, such as a family allowance book or driving licence. There is nothing to pay.

How many items you can borrow

It is usually up to twenty books at any one time. There are separate limits for other media. Please ask for our current leaflet on hiring CDs, videos, DVDs, audio cassettes and CD-Roms.

How long you can keep them

Normally three weeks for books. Other media are hired by the week. The date of return is stamped on the date label.

If you haven't finished with them

You can renew books by telephone, post, by using the online borrower services or at the library unless someone else is waiting for them. You must pay an additional hire charge for other media.

What it costs

Most services are free. We charge for special requests.

Did you know ...?

In the English-speaking world there are more than 2,800 public libraries. The Public Libraries Act of 1850 enabled towns in the UK to spend rates (now council tax) on libraries, which anyone in the district could use free of charge. Borrowing has remained free to this day. Libraries are run by local councils, and you can find out about them on council websites.

3 Look at the questions you wrote in Exercise 1. Does this leaflet answer your questions? Write the answers if you can.

a ....
....
b ....
....
c ....
....

4 Select three other pieces of information from the website to tell a friend about the library services. Use your own words.

....
....
....

....
....
....

....
....
....

E X tra practice

If you are living in an English-speaking country, find out about joining your local library. Some libraries have a section of books for English language students like yourself. Why not find out what is available and borrow one of these books? If you are not living in an English-speaking country, you can still probably borrow English books.

B Paying for library services

1 In the text in Section A, you read that borrowing books from libraries is free. Did the website say anything about what you have to pay for?

2 Look at the three things on the right (a–c) that libraries ask you to pay for. Imagine you are telling a friend. Complete the sentences in your own words.

a [You have to pay ....]

b [You have to pay ....]

c [You have to pay ....]

3 Skim the three leaflets on this page. Match the headings (a–c) in Exercise 2 with the leaflets (1–3). How quickly can you match them?

a ☐ b ☐ c ☐

a **OVERDUE CHARGES FOR BOOKS**

b **RESERVATION CHARGES**

c **AUDIO VISUAL HIRE SERVICES**

1

CHARGES		PRICE BANDS				
PER ITEM		1	2	3	4	5
		yellow spot	green spot	red spot	blue spot	gold star
VIDEO	per week	£1	–	£2	£3	£3.50
DVD	"	£1	–	£2	£3	£3.50
CD-ROM	"	£1	£1.50	£2	£3	–
MUSIC CD	"	£1	£1.50	£2	£3	–
AUDIO BOOK per 3 weeks		75p	£1.50	£1.50	–	–
LANGUAGE PACK	"	£1	£1.50	–	–	–

The AUDIO BOOK service is FREE to visually impaired people, to people with dyslexia or who have a disability which prevents them from using printed books, and to children in public care.

Up to 5 items in each category may be hired. There are no concessionary rates. Staff reserve the right to exercise discretion in issuing videos and DVDs carrying 12, 15 and 18 certificates.

These hire services are not available in every library. However, items may be obtained through the reservation service, in which case a hire charge is payable in addition to the reservation fee.

2

Books may usually be borrowed for three weeks. Fines are charged on books which are kept beyond the date due for return. The purpose of fines is to encourage the prompt return of books in order to ensure that the maximum use is made of the book stock.

Overdue charges will not be applied to books borrowed by readers registered as house-bound or chronically sick and disabled.

The following charges will be made on each book returned late:

	Adults	Under 18s
Per day for first week	15p	5p
2nd week or part week overdue	£1.50	50p
Rising at weekly intervals by	60p	20p
To a maximum of	£6.30	£2.30

3

Standard rate 70p   Concessions 35p
(payable when reservation is made)

Concessionary rates apply to persons who are:
under 18 years of age
chronically sick and disabled

A reservation fee of 70p will be charged to your account if you reserve online unless you are eligible for the concessionary rate. The fee will be payable on your next library visit.

You will be notified by post when your reserved item is available for collection. If you no longer want an item that you have reserved, please contact your local library. It is not possible to cancel a reservation online. We regret that the reservation fee is not refundable.

4 **Read what members of staff said to six library users. Are the users coming into the library (C), or are they going out (G)?**

a [This book was due back two days ago. There's 30 pence to pay.] ..C..

b [Both DVDs are red spot, so that's £4.00. They're due back a week today.] ------ c [These two books are a week late. That's £3.00.] ------

d [That's 75 pence, and you can have it for three weeks.] ------

e [If you want to reserve the book, it'll cost 70 pence.] ------ f [I'm afraid you can't have six CDs.] ------

5 **What exactly are the users in Exercise 4 doing? Complete these sentences.**

a He / She's *returning a book which is late.* _____
b He / She's _____
c He / She's _____
d He / She's _____
e He / She's _____
f He / She's _____

6 **Scan the leaflets on the opposite page again and <u>underline</u> the information which confirms what the members of staff are saying in Exercise 4.**

Class bonus

Look at the list of overdue charges and audio visual hire services. Write some sentences like sentences a–d in Exercise 4 – but leave out the charges. Exchange your sentences with another student. Can you complete your friend's sentences with the correct charges?

7 **Look at the questions you wrote in Exercise 1 in Section A. Do these leaflets answer any more of your questions? Write the answers in Exercise 3 in Section A if you can.**

Focus on ...
word families

Find two or more related words in the leaflets on the opposite page which start with these letters. Are the words nouns (N), verbs (V) or adjectives (A)?

a char *ges (N) charged (V)* _____
b disab _____
c hir _____
d conce _____
e res _____
f ret _____

Find words in the leaflets which are related to these words. Decide whatw part of speech both words are.

g week *(N) weekly (A)* _____
h print _____
i pay _____
j follow _____
k collect _____
l refund _____

Complete these sentences with six of the words from the leaflets.

m My glasses weren't ready when I went to the optician's, so I had to go back the _____*following*_____ day.
n There are special seats on buses for elderly and _____ people.
o If you've got a student card, you can usually get _____ on ticket prices.
p This ticket is non-_____ – you can't get your money back.
q Your washing will be ready for _____ at seven o'clock.
r I'm seeing Jon on Tuesday for my _____ private lesson.

Can-do checklist

Tick what you can do.

	Can do	Need more practice
I can put the sentences of a text into my own words.	✓	✓
I can find out about a library, what I can borrow and what I have to pay for.	✓	✓

Unit 14
At the sports centre

Get ready to read

- What are these different sports and physical activities? Write the name of each activity.
  a ___circuit training___
  b _____
  c _____
  d _____
  e _____
  f _____

  a   b   c   d   e   f

- How many other sports and physical activities can you name?

- How many of these sports and physical activities have you tried?

- Tick ✓ the sentences that are true for you.
  I don't like sport or physical exercise. ☐
  I do sport or physical exercise more than three times a week. ☐
  I am on a sports team. ☐
  I belong to a sports club. ☐
  I go to the local sports centre. ☐
  I do sport with people I work/study with. ☐

go to Useful language p. 86

A I don't fancy playing

Learning tip

We skim some texts – read quickly to get the general sense. We scan other texts – read quickly to find a particular piece of information. Sometimes we can combine these two approaches to reading: skimming first to get the general sense and then scanning for a specific point.

1 Nobu has just started working for a company in Cambridge which has its own sports centre. Skim the noticeboard on the opposite page. Can Nobu only do sports at the sports centre?

2 Nobu is interested in doing some physical exercise. Scan the noticeboard and answer these questions.
  a Which activities are weekly classes? _____
  b Which sports activity is not a class? _____
  c Which notice is for a class that might take place?
  ----

3 What could Nobu do at lunchtimes? Scan the noticeboard again and write short notes.

  ----

4 Someone has told Nobu that there is football once a week. Answer Nobu's questions about football in no more than three words.
  a Which day is it? _____
  b At what time? _____
  c Who should he contact for more information?
  ----

5 Nobu is not sure that he is good enough to play football. Read the same notice again. <u>Underline</u> the words in these sentences so that they are true.
  a The notice *mentions / doesn't mention* how good you need to be.
  b He *would have to play / wouldn't have to play* if he went along this week.

The Sports Centre

Algerian cultural night

Featuring the Rai band *Nassim*

Friday 5th May at 7pm

in the Sports Centre

Tickets are available from Rashid Amrani (ext 6721) and cost £10 which includes traditional Algerian buffet.

All proceeds to be donated to victims of the recent Algerian earthquake.

New Salsa Workshop!

Place: Sports Centre
Date: Thursday 4th May
Time: 6:30 – 9:30pm
Fee: £10 per person
Clothing: comfortable shoes and loose clothes
Bring plenty of water (energy snacks will be provided)

The workshop will give a thorough grounding in all basic salsa moves, and hopes to bring people up to a beginner – intermediate level.

No need to bring a partner.

For further information please contact Maria-José Luque on Ext. 6266

Yoga continues

A course of 5 lunchtime sessions for anyone, whether new to yoga or with some experience.
When: Monday 12.30 – 1.30pm
Where: Sports Centre – Squash court 2
Instructor: Sissel Fowler
Cost: £20 for 5 sessions
To make a booking or a query: please contact Jane Norman – Ext 7543. If you have questions about style or strength of the yoga, please email sissel@virgin.net.

Aerobics Class with Pam Eyton – Wednesday Lunchtimes

Wednesday lunchtimes from 12.30pm – 1.15pm in Squash Court 2.
Price £3 per session. All abilities welcome.
For further information please contact Judy Shakespeare on ext. 3342

Circuit training

Why not try a circuit class? It involves no coordination!

A fun overall body workout and you can work to your own level

At the Sports Centre in Squash Court 2 from 12.15pm – 1.00pm, every Thursday
£3.00 per person per class

For more information, please contact Alan McLean on ext. 2145

MIXED 5-A-SIDE FOOTBALL

MIXED FOOTBALL ON THE ASTROTURF EVERY TUESDAY 4.30PM TO 6PM. EVERYONE WELCOME. IF YOU DON'T FANCY PLAYING, WHY NOT COME ALONG AND WATCH?

CONTACT JOHN CURRIE ON EXT 2347

Pilates

Would you like to strengthen, lengthen and realign your body?
Do you need to improve your posture, body shape and sports performance?
Could you participate in an exercise method that links the mind and the body?
If so, Pilates could be for you. If you're interested in taking part in lunchtime Pilates lessons in the Sports Centre, please contact Richard Hammond on ext 4351.

Focus on …
–ing forms 1

Words ending in *–ing* which are formed from verbs can be verbs, nouns or adjectives. The word *featuring* in the Algerian cultural night notice is a verb – it comes from the verb *feature* which means 'include someone or something as an important part'.

a Find six more *–ing* forms in the notices. Decide if each word is part of a verb (V) or a noun (N).

_____clothing_____ [N]   _____ ☐   _____ ☐
_____ ☐   _____ ☐   _____ ☐

Complete these sentences with the words above. Some of the words can be both verbs and nouns. Decide if each word is a verb (V) or a noun (N).

b I haven't been _____playing_____ much tennis recently. [V]
c I'm interested in _____ a tennis court. ☐
d The race is next week. I've spent ages _____ for it. ☐
e The course gave me a good _____ in posture and body shape. ☐
f Make sure you bring warm _____ for the walk. ☐
g Do you fancy _____ part in a 10-kilometre run for charity? ☐

6 What sports activity would you do if you worked for the same company as Nobu? Would you be interested in any of the other activities?

Class bonus

Work with a partner. One of you has just joined the company and the other is the sports centre manager. Ask and answer questions about the notices on the noticeboard.

B It's a racquet game

1 Look at the photograph on the right. What is this sport? Have you ever played it?

2 Nobu has never played squash, but he would like to try. Scan the sports centre notice and answer these questions.

a Is it possible for him to try this new sport? yes

b When? _____

c Where? _____

d Could he have lessons?

_____

e When? _____

f Where? _____

g How much would they cost?

_____

Squash Club at the Sports Centre

New members and new players of all abilities are always welcome.

Friday evening is squash club night from 5.30pm onwards – come and join us in the Sports Centre for a game and a drink.

For further information please contact first team captain Arthur Smith on ext 5381.

Squash Coaching at the Sports Centre

Are you interested in participating in Squash Coaching Sessions? All standards are welcome.

Rachel Brookes is a fully qualified England Squash Level 2 Coach and will be offering her services to staff and selected guests as a squash coach in the near future.

Times of coaching sessions are flexible. For instance, they could be offered at lunchtimes and straight after work, depending on demand. Individual coaching sessions or group sessions could be arranged. Prices will be £20 per hour for one person, and £5 extra for each additional person.

3 Nobu also sees an advert for real tennis. He asks himself the same questions as in Exercise 2. Find the answers to the questions.

Real Tennis

A compelling opportunity
this summer at Grange Road, Cambridge

Your chance to enjoy Real Tennis, the king of racquet sports, starts on 6th July with the World Champion.

6.30pm – 8.00pm, 6 July

A wonderful introductory evening with Rob Fahey, world champion and widely regarded as the greatest player ever.

Including an exciting exhibition match: The World Champion vs The British Amateur Champion, David Woodman.

Plus …
Your turn to play

Friendly expert coaching during a two-hour group lesson to give you the basics, provided by the club's team of first-class professionals at a time to suit you this summer, with racquets and balls provided. It's indoors, so there is no chance of being rained off!

A lasting memento

A copy of the fascinating book Real Tennis in Cambridge: The First Six Hundred Years to help you to appreciate the place of the game in our great city.

The Real Tennis Club

- Racquets and balls provided
- Ladies' morning
- Teams of all standards competing in national competitions – and winning!
- Club tournaments and club nights suitable for all

Why not become part of this intriguing, rewarding and entertaining world?

Come and try this fascinating sport this summer – by yourself, with friends, or as a family. All are welcome.

Extraordinary value

The whole introductory package – introductory evening, book, and group lesson – is just £50 per person.
For further information or to book your place, contact Manuel Simpson, Head Professional, tel: 01223 357141 email: mani@curtc.net

4 What are the similarities between the squash club and the real tennis club? What are the differences? Complete the chart.

Similarities	Differences
both clubs have club nights	

Focus on ...
–*ing* forms 2

The word *compelling* in the first line of the real tennis advert is an adjective. Find the other adjectives ending in –*ing* in the advertisement. Complete the words.

1 a e x c i t i n g
  b f _ _ _ _ _ _ _ _ _ _
  c i _ _ _ _ _ _ _ _ _
  d r _ _ _ _ _ _ _ _
  e e _ _ _ _ _ _ _ _ _ _

2 Match the beginnings and endings of these sentences.

a I had to finish the book in one go –   1 it's quite an intriguing game.
b The film made me laugh –   2 but it's also very rewarding.
c Learning English is hard work –   3 it is so compelling.
d I love films about real people –   4 it was quite entertaining.
e I've always been interested in chess –   5 I find them absolutely fascinating.

Which three adjectives in the exercise above mean 'very, very interesting'?

5 Would you rather try squash at the sports club or real tennis at Grange Road? Why?

Did you know ...?

Real tennis is also called *royal* or *court tennis*. It is a game played indoors with racquets and balls and a net in an area which looks like a courtyard. It was very popular with royalty and nobility in the 16th century. Today there are only about 45 real tennis courts in the world. The more modern game of tennis (or *lawn tennis*) quickly became more popular than real tennis at the beginning of the twentieth century. Modern tennis took on the same system of scoring, where zero is 'love' and one is 'fifteen'.

E✗tra practice

Find out more about squash or real tennis. Do some research in a library or on the Internet. You could try www.wisegeek.com or www.real-tennis.nl.

Can-do checklist

Tick what you can do.

	Can do	Need more practice
I can use a variety of approaches when reading texts.	✓	✓
I can read advertisements on a noticeboard and decide what I am interested in.		✓
I can find out about taking up a new sport and having lessons.	✓	

Unit 15
I'd like to work here

go to Useful language p. 86

Get ready to read

○ Which of these things are the most important to you in a job?
Put them in order. (1 = most important, 6 = least important)

colleagues ☐   holidays ☐   hours ☐   location ☐
pay ☐   training and development opportunities ☐

○ Look at these products. What are they?

a books
b _____
c _____
d _____
e _____
f _____

○ Imagine you decide to get a job in a shop. Which of the products in the pictures would you be interested in selling?

A Job profiles

1 In this unit you are going to read some texts from a company website. Scan the webpage below and complete these sentences.

a The name of the company is _____ .
b It sells _____ .

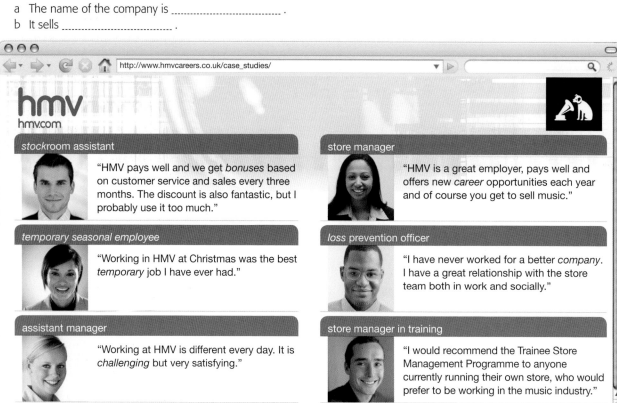

http://www.hmvcareers.co.uk/case_studies/

hmv
hmv.com

stockroom assistant
"HMV pays well and we get *bonuses* based on customer service and sales every three months. The discount is also fantastic, but I probably use it too much."

temporary seasonal employee
"Working in HMV at Christmas was the best *temporary* job I have ever had."

assistant manager
"Working at HMV is different every day. It is *challenging* but very satisfying."

store manager
"HMV is a great employer, pays well and offers new *career* opportunities each year and of course you get to sell music."

loss prevention officer
"I have never worked for a better *company*. I have a great relationship with the store team both in work and socially."

store manager in training
"I would recommend the Trainee Store Management Programme to anyone currently running their own store, who would prefer to be working in the music industry."

2 Skim what the people say on the webpage. Do they like working for this company?

Learning tip

When you are reading, you can use either a dictionary with English and your language or a dictionary which has definitions in English. The main advantage of using this second type of dictionary is that you are working in English all the time. Another benefit is they contain lots of examples of how words are used.

3 Scan the webpage and find the words in *italics*. Do you know what they mean? There is not much context to help you, so if you do not know the meaning of the words, use the entries below from the *Cambridge Learner's English Dictionary*.

benefit¹ /'benɪfɪt/ *noun* [C, U] **1** something that helps you or gives you an advantage *I've had the benefit of a happy childhood.*

bonus /'bəʊnəs/ *noun* [C] **1** an extra amount of money that you are given, especially because you have worked hard *All employees received a bonus of £500.*

career¹ /kə'rɪəʳ/ *noun* [C] **1** a job that you do for a long period of your life and that gives you the chance to move to a higher position and earn more money *a successful career in mar-*

◦▪company /'kʌmpəni/ *noun* **1** BUSINESS [C] an organization which sells goods or services *a software/telephone company*

employee /ɪm'plɔɪiː/ *noun* [C] someone who is paid to work for a person or company

◦▪loss /lɒs/ *noun* **1** NOT HAVING [C, U] when you do not have someone or something that you had before, or when you have less of something than before *loss of income/memory* ○ *blood/hair/weight loss* ○ *job losses*

◦▪product /'prɒdʌkt/ *noun* [C] **1** something that is made or grown to be sold *They have a new range of skin-care products.*

pension¹ /'penʃən/ *noun* [C] money that is paid regularly by the government or a private company to a person who has stopped working because they are old or ill

retail¹ /'riːteɪl/ *noun* [U] when products are sold to customers from shops *jobs in retail*

seasonal /'siːzənəl/ *adjective* happening or existing only at a particular time of the year *a seasonal worker* ○ *the seasonal migration of birds*

stock¹ /stɒk/ *noun* **1** SHOP [U] all the goods that are available in a shop *We're expecting some new stock in this afternoon.*

◦▪structure¹ /'strʌktʃəʳ/ *noun* **1** [C, U] the way that parts of something are arranged or put together

temporary /'tempərəri/ *adjective* existing or happening for only a short or limited time *a temporary job*

Focus on ...
job and *work*

The words *job* and *work* are often confused by students of English. Underline the correct word in each sentence. Then check your answers in the webpage on the opposite page.

a 'Working in HMV at Christmas was the best temporary *job / work* I have ever had.'

b 'I have a great relationship with the store team both in *job / work* and socially.'

Complete these sentences with *job*, *jobs* or *work*. Note that *work* is uncountable – you cannot say *a work*.

c I've got a new .... in the personnel department.

d Hundreds of people might lose their ....

e I go to .... by public transport.

f Teaching must be an interesting ....

4 Skim the webpage again. In which job are you most likely to sell directly to customers?

5 Look at the webpage below. Use the dictionary entries again if you need to. In your opinion, what are the most important benefits of working for this company? (1 = most important, 6 = least important) Write the numbers in the boxes.

a ☐ b ☐ c ☐ d ☐ e ☐ f ☐

○ ○ ○

http://www.hmvcareers.co.uk/store_careers/benefits.asp

hmv
hmv.com

store careers: benefits

a One of the highest rates of pay in *retail*

b Quarterly bonus scheme

c 30% *product* discount

d 23 days paid holiday – we ask that you don't take holidays in December, our busiest time of year

e Company *pension* scheme

f *Structured* development and training

6 Scan the first webpage again. Answer these questions about benefits.

a Which benefits does the stockroom assistant mention?

----

b Which of the benefits do the other employees mention?

----

7 Would you like to work for HMV? Why? / Why not?

B There are jobs available

1 In this section, you are going to read two job profiles. Look at the job titles. What do you think people with these job titles do?

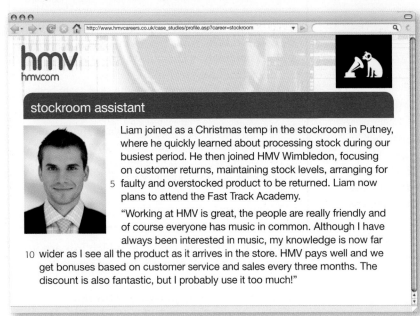

stockroom assistant

Liam joined as a Christmas temp in the stockroom in Putney, where he quickly learned about processing stock during our busiest period. He then joined HMV Wimbledon, focusing on customer returns, maintaining stock levels, arranging for
5 faulty and overstocked product to be returned. Liam now plans to attend the Fast Track Academy.

"Working at HMV is great, the people are really friendly and of course everyone has music in common. Although I have always been interested in music, my knowledge is now far
10 wider as I see all the product as it arrives in the store. HMV pays well and we get bonuses based on customer service and sales every three months. The discount is also fantastic, but I probably use it too much!"

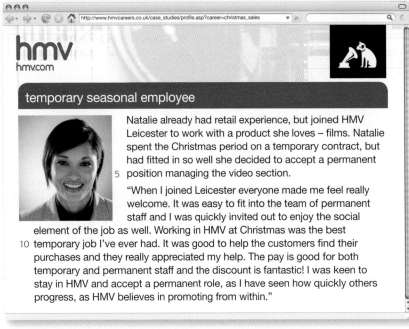

temporary seasonal employee

Natalie already had retail experience, but joined HMV Leicester to work with a product she loves – films. Natalie spent the Christmas period on a temporary contract, but had fitted in so well she decided to accept a permanent
5 position managing the video section.

"When I joined Leicester everyone made me feel really welcome. It was easy to fit into the team of permanent staff and I was quickly invited out to enjoy the social element of the job as well. Working in HMV at Christmas was the best
10 temporary job I've ever had. It was good to help the customers find their purchases and they really appreciated my help. The pay is good for both temporary and permanent staff and the discount is fantastic! I was keen to stay in HMV and accept a permanent role, as I have seen how quickly others progress, as HMV believes in promoting from within."

2 Read the two profiles. Which of the people do these sentences describe? It could be Liam, Natalie or both of them. Circle one or both words.

a *He / She* started work at HMV as a temporary seasonal employee.

b *He / She* still works in the same store.

c *He / She* is now a manager.

d *He / She* gets on really well with the other staff.

e *He / She* is less interested in music than films.

f *He / She* buys things from HMV.

3 Look at the sentences in Exercise 2 which describe only one of the people. Decide why these sentences are *not* true for the other person and write true sentences.

Liam _____

_____

_____

_____

_____

_____

_____

_____

_____

_____

_____

4 Read the profiles again. Write your answers to these questions.

a When exactly is HMV's *busiest period*? (lines 3–4)

_____

b Overstocked product has *to be returned*. Where do you think it has to be returned to? (lines 6–7)

_____

c Natalie had *retail experience*. What do you think this means? (line 1)

_____

d What is the *social element* of the job? (line 9)

_____

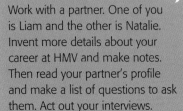

Class bonus

Work with a partner. One of you is Liam and the other is Natalie. Invent more details about your career at HMV and make notes. Then read your partner's profile and make a list of questions to ask them. Act out your interviews.

5 Look at the webpage on the right. Liam plans to attend the Fast Track Academy. What positions could he get at the end of his training?

----

6 Look at the list of positions. Select the role you would be most interested in.

http://www.hmvcareers.co.uk/store_careers/

hmv
hmv.com

store careers opportunities:

As the leading music, DVD and games retailer in the UK and Ireland we are looking for bright, energetic and committed individuals.

We can offer you excellent pay and benefits, as well as structured training and development that can lead to exciting career opportunities within our stores. Nearly all of our Team Leaders, Assistant Managers and Store Managers have been promoted internally through our structured Development and Fast Track programmes.

The following positions are all available at HMV; please select the role you are interested in for further information:

- Temporary Seasonal Employee
- Sales Assistant (Full-time and weekend)
- Loss Prevention Officer
- Stockroom Assistant
- Cash Office Assistant (Full-time and part-time)

Did you know ...?

HMV stands for 'His Master's Voice' and is the name of a painting by Francis Barraud. Originally HMV was known as the Gramophone Company; it was started in 1898, to import gramophones and gramophone records from Germany into Britain. By the end of the year, it was making its own recordings. The company bought the picture, asked Barraud to repaint the gramophone so that the dog was listening to one of its own gramophones, and has used the image ever since as a logo.

E✗tra practice

Read the texts in Section B again. Try and work out the meaning of any words you do not know. If you can't work out their meaning, look for help in a dictionary with English definitions.

Can-do checklist

Tick what you can do.

	Can do	Need more practice
I can use a dictionary with English definitions to find out the meaning of words.	✓	✓
I can find out about jobs and benefits on a company website.	✓	✓
I can choose a job I am interested in.		

Unit 16
Just the job!

go to Useful language p. 86

Get ready to read

○ Imagine you need to change job or get a job. How would you try and find a job? Tick ✓ the methods you would use.
I'd ask my friends if there were any opportunities where they worked. ☐
I'd write to companies I'd like to work for. ☐
I'd look at adverts in the newspaper. ☐
I'd search on the Internet. ☐
I'd look at adverts in shop windows. ☐
I'd go into places and ask about work opportunities. ☐

○ Imagine you are studying in York (perhaps you are!). What kind of job would you look for if you needed some extra money? Complete the sentence.
I'd like to *be / work* ....

A Can you start immediately?

1 **Blanca is from Argentina. It is the end of June and she is studying English in York. She is hoping to find a job for two or three hours a day. She thinks she might be able to use her first language. What is her first language? Tick ✓ one of the boxes.**

a Italian ☐
b Portuguese ☐
c Spanish ☐

Learning tip

We often skim a text – look at it quickly – to find the part of the text which is most useful to us. We can then ignore the rest of the text and focus on the important part. We read the important part slowly, and we probably read some words/phrases/sentences more than once in order to understand the details.

2 **Scan the advertisements from a newspaper on the opposite page. Are there any jobs in which Blanca could use her first language? Which jobs?**

Did you know …?

If something is *just the job*, it is exactly what you want or need. If you say something is *just the job*, you are probably not talking about work! A cup of coffee in the morning, for example, could be just the job if you are tired, thirsty or bored!

3 **Read the last two advertisements carefully. Which advertisement gives the following information?**

a the name of the company/person offering the job 8
b the money you will earn ☐
c the number of hours a week you will work ☐
d the time of day when you'll be working ☐
e the phone number of the contact person ☐

4 **Blanca decides that the two jobs are no good for her. Imagine you are Blanca. Write a list of the possible reasons why the jobs are no good.**

I don't want to work from home. I want to mix with other people. ....
....
....
....
....

5 **Blanca decides to read the other advertisements. What exactly are the jobs?**

1 Library Assistant   4 ....
2 ....   5 ....
3 ....   6 ....

1

Fulford Library

has a vacancy for a Saturday
Library Assistant Two Saturdays
per month
9.30am – 1.00pm

We are also looking for someone to
work alternate Thursday afternoons
2–5pm

Starting salary £7.18 per hour
Application forms available at the
counter
Closing date 9 July

2

Administrator, Publishing in Clifton

**£6.50 p/hr (3 hrs a day – mornings,
Monday to Friday)**

Large publishing organisation seeks
an enthusiastic and committed
team member to provide basic
administration support, deal with post,
distribute post and payslips, organise
travel accommodation for the team.
You will have previous experience
using Word, Excel and Outlook.

CVs to j.lawrie@actionrecruit.co.uk

3

IT Technician
(Non-teaching)

Required to support the ICT
department and the school network, a
well motivated IT technician. Applicants
offering full-time, flexitime or part-time
hours will be welcome.

Letter of application, full CV and
details of two referees should be sent
to the Headmistress by the closing
date of Friday 22nd July.

THE ORATORY SCHOOL OUSEBURN
TERRACE YORK YO20 4EE

Telephone: 01904 241291 –
email: headmistress@oratoryyork.org

Further details available on the
website: www.oratoryyork.org

4

Temporary gardeners needed,
July – end September

Minimum period: 4 weeks
40 hours a week, flexible working hours
No previous knowledge or experience
needed, training given

Apply   **Poppleton Garden Centre,
York 01904 347652**

5

Seasonal workers needed for
fruit picking and packing
Accommodation provided,
good rates of pay
Phone 01423 783565

6

We need happy, hardworking
bar and floor staff. Part-time
or full-time, evenings and
weekends. Good tips and
good fun. Call Chris or Gail on
09675 433423

7

**Can you read Spanish?
Familiar with Microsoft Office?**

11 hours per week from home
£7.69 per hour
01904 408305

8

**Hotel receptionist required
evenings:** experience and
knowledge with both fluent
English and one foreign
language. Enquiries@
marlborohotel.co.uk

---

6 Underline these words in the advertisements.
What do you think they mean?

a full-time, part-time, flexitime
b temporary, seasonal

Focus on ...
vocabulary

There are lots of useful words in the first three
advertisements about applying for jobs. Complete the
definitions of some of the words.

a A ____vacancy____ is a job that is available.
b Your _____ is a fixed amount of money that
you get from your employer.
c An _____ is a document that you use
officially to ask for a job.
d The _____ is the last day on which you can
apply for a job.
e Your _____ is a document describing your
qualifications and the jobs that you have done, which
you send to an employer that you want to work for.
f A _____ is someone who knows you well
and writes a letter to say if you are suitable for a job.

7 Some advertisements do not include the
words in Exercise 6. Which of the words
could you use to describe the jobs in those
advertisements?

1 Fulford Library Assistant = part-time
_____
_____
_____
_____

8 How do you apply for the jobs? Complete the
sentences with the job numbers.

a You apply for jobs _____ in writing.
b You phone someone about jobs _____ .

9 Which of the jobs would be good for these
people? Write the job numbers. (Sometimes
more than one job would be good.)

a someone who likes being outdoors ___4, 5___
b someone who is doing a full-time English course
_____
c someone who knows a lot about computers _____
d someone who only wants to work a few hours a month
_____

B I'm going to apply

1 Which of these things do job application forms usually ask for? Tick ✓ the boxes.

a your personal details ☐

b your educational qualifications ☐

c details of other jobs you have done ☐

d details about your health ☐

e details about your hobbies and interests ☐

f the names of two referees ☐

g your reasons for thinking you would be good at the job ☐

h your reasons for wanting to work for the company ☐

CALLED TO THE BAR

Called To The Bar opened in 2006 with the aim of providing its customers with fine food and wine. We are always looking for staff who can help us to do this. If you're interested in working for us, then we're interested in hearing from you.

Please complete the following using BLOCK CAPITALS:

POSITION APPLIED FOR: .... Full-time ☐ Part-time ☐

What attracted you to Called To The Bar? ....

What do you think you can bring to Called To The Bar? ....

Name .... Title (Mr / Mrs / Ms / Miss)

Address ....

.... Postcode ....

Telephone number .... Marital status .... Date of Birth ....

National Insurance Number .... Do you have a valid work permit? (if applicable) YES ☐ NO ☐

PLEASE GIVE DETAILS OF YOUR CURRENT AND PREVIOUS EMPLOYMENT, COVERING THE LAST 3 YEARS

Name and address of Employer	Dates employed from / until	Position Held	Duties	FT/PT	Reason for leaving

PLEASE ANSWER THE FOLLOWING QUESTIONS (Tick the correct answer and comment where applicable)

PERIOD	YES	NO	PERIOD	YES	NO
Lunchtimes			Weekends		
Evenings			Public Holidays		

If you've answered NO to any of the above, please specify when you will not be able to work.

....

1 How will you travel to work? ....

2 Do you have experience and/or qualifications relevant to this business? YES ☐ NO ☐
  (If YES, please give details) ....

3 Which, if any, additional help/facilities will you require to enable you to carry out your duties? e.g. wheelchair access

....

4 What commitments do you have outside work? ....

EQUAL OPPORTUNITIES

It is the policy of Called To The Bar that there shall be no discrimination in respect of sex, marital status, colour, creed, race, nationality and ethnic or national origin, disability, political or religious beliefs, and that equal opportunities shall be given to all employees. In order to ensure the effectiveness of our Equal Opportunities policy, it would be of great help if you would tick the appropriate box. It is not, however, compulsory to complete this section and it will not affect your chances of selection if you choose not to do so. Please tick the appropriate ethnic/racial group to which you belong.

Afro-Caribbean ☐ Asian ☐ European White ☐ Other ☐

PLEASE GIVE THE NAME AND ADDRESS OF TWO PEOPLE WHO CAN BE CONTACTED FOR A REFERENCE (WORK-RELATED IF POSSIBLE)

1 Name ....

  Address .... Telephone ....

2 Name ....

  Address .... Telephone ....

PLEASE COMPLETE THE FOLLOWING

I understand that any inaccuracy or falsification of the information I have given may result in termination of my employment.

I have completed this form personally and declare that the above information is true in all respects.

Signed .... Date ....

2 Skim the application form on the opposite page. What kind of vacancies do you think this company might have? Complete the sentence.

There might be vacancies for _____ .

3 Which of the things in Exercise 1 does the application form ask for? Put the things in the order they are mentioned.

1 ☐   2 ☐   3 ☐   4 ☐   5 ☐

4 What other things does the form ask about? Why do you think it asks about these things? Complete the sentences.

a It asks about *when exactly you can work (lunchtimes, evenings, etc.)* _____
because Called To The Bar needs to know
when you'll be available to work _____ .

b It asks about _____
_____
because Called To The Bar needs to know
_____
_____ .

c It asks about _____
_____
because Called To The Bar needs to know
_____
_____ .

d It asks about _____
_____
because Called To The Bar needs to know
_____
_____ .

e It asks about _____
_____
because Called To The Bar needs to know
_____
_____ .

5 What things does the application form tell you about? Complete the sentences.

a It tells you about _____ .
b It also tells you about _____ .

6 Choose the job you would most like to do for Called To The Bar and complete the application form. You may need to continue some parts – *previous employment*, for example – on another piece of paper.

Did you know …?

The Commission for Racial Equality (CRE) is a public organization in the UK which deals with racial discrimination and promotes racial equality. It was set up to enforce the Race Relations Act of 1976.

E✗tra practice

Find out the meaning of *to be called to the Bar* from a dictionary. How many other meanings of *bar* are there?

Class bonus

Give your completed application form to another student. Check your partner's form for mistakes. Then discuss your forms together. Whose answers are better, do you think?

Can-do checklist

Tick what you can do.

	Can do	Need more practice
I can skim a page of advertisements in a newspaper to find out which ones are most useful to me.	✓	✓
I can understand job advertisements and choose a job which suits me.		
I can complete a job application form.		

A Are these statements true (T) or false (F)?

1 Information is the only thing you can get from reading a text. ...... (Unit 12)
2 If you have to understand a difficult piece of text, try and put the sentences into your own words. ...... (Unit 13)
3 You usually skim a text before you scan it. ...... (Unit 14)
4 You often find lots of examples in a dictionary which has translations in your own language. ...... (Unit 15)
5 Once you have identified the important part of a text, you will only need to read it again quickly. ...... (Unit 16)

B Now read the *Learning tips* for Units 12–16 on pages 90–91. Do you want to change any of your answers in Exercise A?

C Skim the five texts on these pages. Decide which text these people would read. Write the letter of the text in the box.

6 someone who wants to do some exercise ☐
7 someone who applied for a job ☐
8 someone who wants to find a job ☐
9 someone who wants to send an email ☐
10 someone who wants to check their spelling ☐

Text A

1 –able
a Add –able to words which make sense on their own.
able + drink = drinkable
able + adapt = adaptable
b Use –able after a hard "c" or hard "g".
educable navigable amicable [The "c" and "g" here are hard letters.]
c Drop the "e" when you add –able to a word that ends in "e".
value + able = valuable

2 –ible
a Add –ible to letters that do not make sense on their own.
sens + ible = sensible
vis + ible = visible
b Add –ible to most words with "s" or "ss" before the ending.
responsible permissible
c Use –ible after a soft "c" or soft "g".
legible eligible invincible [The "g" and "c" here are soft letters.]

Text B

Length of stay

In fairness to all, use of library computers is limited to a maximum of 60 minutes per user per day, subject to availability. Use of some computers is restricted to 15 or 30 minute sessions, and on these computers the daily maximum may be spread over more than one session. If nobody else is waiting, staff may at their discretion allow you to stay on a computer for longer than the allotted time, but you must leave it once it is required by another user. You must leave your computer at the end of your allotted time and when requested to do so by library staff. Booking systems are in operation at many libraries.

Before you leave your terminal, you must click on the 'End Session' icon, and follow the simple onscreen instructions. This clears all your work from the computer. If you do not do this, your work may be viewed by the next user.

Please note that computers will be unavailable for the last 15 minutes before the library closes.

Use of computers is free of charge, but printing costs 20p per A4 sheet (black or colour). Please click on the Print button only if you wish to buy a print.

Text C

Oasis Sports Centre

Bookings and cancellations – Members can book most activities up to six days in advance. Non-members can book most activities up to five days in advance but must pay at the time of booking. 48 hours notice is required for cancellations. Failure to comply or no-shows will result in the full charge being made.

Personal Belongings – Bags are not allowed in activity areas and must not be left unattended.

Lockers – Lockers are available for your belongings at all centres. £1 refundable, £0.20 non-refundable.

Facilities include:
Indoor/Outdoor Swimming Pool
Fitness Centre
Group Exercise Classes
Squash
Café

Opening hours
Monday – Friday 6.30am – 10pm
Saturday – Sunday 9.30am – 6.00pm

Text D

```
┌─────────────────────────────────────────────┐
│ ○○○                                          │
│ ◄ ► C +  [_____] ▼ Q-      │
├─────────────────────────────────────────────┤
```

Job Title   Administrator
Salary/Rate   £7.67 per hour
Location   Liverpool
Job Type   TEMP
Job reference 4475432

[SEND TO A FRIEND] [ADD TO BASKET] [APPLY FOR JOB]

Description
An enthusiastic individual with a lively personality and good communication skills is needed on a temporary basis to cover sick leave. Main responsibilities include: entering information into database, filing and photocopying, taking calls and basic administrative tasks. Applicants must be available for an immediate start and be IT literate.

Benefits
Canteen, free parking

Text E

Dear Ms Maldini,

APPOINTMENT OF JUNIOR SALES ASSISTANT

Thank you very much for attending an interview last week.

We had an enormous response to our advertisement. This meant that it was very hard to choose just one person from the many applicants, yourself included, who had the experience, qualifications and personality we were looking for.

We wish you every success in finding a suitable position. If, in the future, we advertise another vacancy, please feel free to apply. We will be very happy to consider your application.

Yours sincerely,

Kylie Graham (Mrs)
PERSONNEL MANAGER, WRIGHT'S STORE

D Read the rules in Text A. Tick ✓ the correct word in each pair. You will find only two of the words in the text.

11 sensable ☐   sensible ☐
12 valueable ☐   valuable ☐
13 payable ☐   payible ☐
14 impossible ☐   impossable ☐

E A friend tells you about using the library computers. Read Text B and decide if what your friend says is true (T) or false (F).

15 Sometimes you can only use a computer for quarter of an hour. ....
16 If nobody is waiting to use a computer, you can use it for an extra hour. ....
17 You must click on the 'End Session' icon before you begin work. ....
18 If you click on the print button, you will have to pay 20p. ....

F Read Text C. You have joined the sports centre and you decide to book a squash court for the following Sunday. Answer the questions. Write two or three words.

19 What's the earliest time you can play? ....
20 Which day must you cancel if you can't play and you want your money back? ....
21 Where can you put your sports bag while you play?
    ....
22 Can you have something to eat after your match?
    ....

G Read the advertisement (Text D). Here are some sentences about Gabi Zilliken. Is the job suitable for her? Write (Y) yes or (N) no.

23 She is looking for a permanent job. ....
24 She does not like using the telephone. ....
25 She has just arrived in Liverpool and has not got a job. ....
26 She has lots of experience using a computer. ....

H Imagine you are Lucia Maldini and you received the letter (Text E). Which of these sentences are true? Write the letters in the boxes.

27–30
☐   ☐   ☐   ☐

a The job on offer was in a shop.
b Lucia was interviewed last week.
c Lots of people applied for the job.
d Working at Wright's is very hard.
e Lucia did not have the right qualifications.
f She has already got another job.
g There is another job available at Wright's.
h Lucia didn't get the job.

Appendix 1
Useful language

This section contains a list of words which are important for carrying out the reading tasks for each unit. You can use the list in three ways.

1 You can look at the list before you begin the unit and make sure that you understand the meaning of the words by looking them up in a dictionary.
2 You can look at the list before you begin the unit, but try and work out the meaning of the words when you meet them in the unit.
3 You can look at the list when you have completed the unit and check that you understand the words.

When you start using the book, you may prefer to use the list in the first way. However, you will find each word in one of the texts, and the context – the words around the unknown word – will help you to work out its meaning. As you develop your reading skills, you will probably realise that it is not necessary to look at the list before you begin the unit. You may already know some of the words; you will be able to work out others from the text or the task.

Each list is a record of the vocabulary of the unit. You can use it as a checklist when you have completed the unit. There is space after each word to write a translation in your own language or an English expression using the word. Mark each word that you understand and can use with a highlighter pen.

There is also space below the wordlist for you to write other words from the unit which are important to you. Look at *Appendix 3* for ideas on what to record for each word.

Unit 1

Reading A
(be within) easy reach *expression* ....
takeaway *noun (+ adjective)* ....
stationer's *noun* ....
store *noun* ....
branch *noun* ....
launderette *noun* ....
dry cleaner's *noun* ....
optician's *noun* ....
bike rental (store) *noun* ....
....
....
....
....
....

Reading B
prescription *noun* ....
maintenance (check) *noun* ....
(For) further information *expression* ....
(on a) voluntary (basis) *adjective* ....
responsibility (for) *noun* ....
donation *noun* ....
....
....
....
....
....

Unit 2

Reading A
packet *noun* ....
package *noun* ....
economical (also economic) *adjective* ....
(non-)urgent *adjective* ....
....
....
....
....
....

Reading B
goods *plural noun* ....
commercial (samples) *adjective* ....
customs *plural noun* ....
form *noun* ....
gift *noun* ....
value *noun* ....
pamphlet *noun* ....
....
....
....
....

Unit 3
Reading A
dance show *expression* ....
musical *noun* ....
hit *noun* ....
performance *noun* ....
(international) tour *noun* ....
tap (dancer) *expression* ....
globe *noun* ....
tenor *noun* ....
production *noun* ....
ovation *noun* ....
....
....
....

Reading B
concession *noun* ....
bank holiday *noun* ....
booking fee *expression* ....
box office *noun* ....
discount *noun* ....
membership *noun* ....
....
....
....
....

Unit 4
Reading A
restriction *noun* ....
cosmetics *plural noun* ....
toiletry *noun* ....
gel *noun* ....
paste *noun* ....
sharp *adjective* ....
dispose of *phrasal verb* ....
cabin baggage *noun* ....
obscure *verb* ....
destination *noun* ....
departure lounge *noun* ....
consume *verb* ....
acquire *verb* ....
....
....
....

Reading B
customs *plural noun* ....
declare *verb* ....
prosecute *verb* ....
allowance *noun* ....
....
....
....

Unit 5
Reading A
ingredients *noun* ....
speciality *noun* ....
savoury *adjective* ....
slice *noun* ....
grilled *adjective* ....
batter *noun* ....
mixture *noun* ....
order *noun* ....
fried *adjective* ....
garnish *noun* ....
tender *adjective* ....
export *verb* ....
....
....
....

Reading B
chalk board *noun* ....
enormous *adjective* ....
reasonably priced *expression* ....
....
....
....

Unit 6
Reading A
downtown *noun* ....
(no) curfew *noun* ....
overall *adjective* ....
rating *noun* ....
atmosphere *noun* ....
budget *noun* ....
kiosk *noun* ....
laundry *noun* ....
bed linen *noun* ....
accommodation *noun* ....
....
....
....

Reading B
valid *adjective* ....
no-show *noun* ....
charge *verb* ....
process *verb* ....
refund *verb* ....
balance *noun* ....
due *adjective* ....
fee *noun* ....
in advance *expression* ....
confirmation *noun* ....
outstanding *adjective* ....
....
....
....

Appendix 1 Useful language

Unit 7

Reading A
cable car *noun* _____
cableway *noun* _____
aerial *adjective* _____
self-service *adjective* _____
_____
_____
_____
_____
_____

Reading B
revolving *adjective* _____
stability *noun* _____
_____
_____
_____
_____
_____
_____

Unit 8

Reading A
package *noun* _____
text *verb* _____
download *verb* _____
unlimited *adjective* _____
network *noun* _____
broadband *noun* _____
landline *noun* _____
off-peak *adjective* _____
_____
_____
_____
_____
_____

Reading B
charge *noun* _____
charge *verb* _____
rate of exchange *expression* _____
dial (direct) *verb* _____
incoming *adjective* _____
prompt *noun* _____
operator *noun* _____
fault *noun* _____
hearing aid (set) *noun* _____
cash *noun* _____
_____
_____
_____
_____
_____

Unit 9

Reading A
graze *noun* _____
treatment *noun* _____
germ *noun* _____
bacteria *noun* _____
wound *noun* _____
infected *adjective* _____
disposable (gloves) *adjective* _____
sterile *adjective* _____
swab *noun* _____
antiseptic (wipes) *adjective* _____
plaster *noun* _____
bandage *noun* _____
casualty *noun* _____
injured *adjective* _____
_____
_____
_____
_____
_____

Reading B
injury *noun* _____
condition *noun* _____
make your own arrangements *expression* _____
dislocation *noun* _____
frustrating *adjective* _____
_____
_____
_____
_____
_____

Unit 10

Reading A
cure *verb* _____
fear *noun* _____
cosmetic surgery *noun* _____
suspension *noun* _____
award *verb* _____
go under the knife *expression* _____
unsightly *adjective* _____
cyst *noun* _____
_____
_____
_____
_____
_____

Reading B
ban *verb* ....
into the red *expression* ....
account *noun* ....
overdrawn *adjective* ....
debit card *noun* ....
(bank) statement *noun* ....
debt *noun* ....
clear a debt *expression* ....
common sense *noun* ....
in line with *expression* ....
trigger *verb* ....
(news)paper round *noun* ....
....
....
....
....
....

Unit 11
Reading A
abbreviation *noun* ....
'smiley' *noun* ....
....
....
....
....
....

Reading B
inbox *noun* ....
give up *verb* ....
work out *verb* ....
unable *adjective* ....
link *noun* ....
....
....
....
....
....

Unit 12
Reading A
individual *adjective* ....
....
....
....

Reading B
wavy *adjective* ....
flag *verb* ....
activate *verb* ....
shortcut *noun* ....
customize *verb* ....
acronym *noun* ....
autocorrect *noun* ....
misspell *verb* ....
....
....
....
....
....

Unit 13
Reading A
browse *verb* ....
application form *noun* ....
confirmation *noun* ....
family allowance book *noun* ....
borrow *verb* ....
current *adjective* ....
hire *verb* ....
renew *verb* ....
....
....
....

Reading B
overdue *adjective* ....
reservation (fee) *noun* ....
visually impaired *expression* ....
disability *noun* ....
public care *expression* ....
concessionary rate *noun* ....
discretion *noun* ....
issue *noun* ....
fine *noun* ....
registered *adjective* ....
eligible *adjective* ....
notify *verb* ....
refundable *adjective* ....
....
....
....
....

Unit 14

Reading A

(not) fancy *verb* _____

cultural night *noun* _____

buffet *noun* _____

workshop *noun* _____

grounding *noun* _____

experience *noun* _____

query *noun* _____

circuit training *noun* _____

coordination *noun* _____

Astroturf *noun* _____

realign *verb* _____

posture *noun* _____

participate in *phrasal verb* _____

_____

_____

_____

_____

_____

Reading B

coaching *noun* _____

session *noun* _____

flexible *adjective* _____

additional *adjective* _____

compelling *adjective* _____

exhibition match *noun* _____

extraordinary *adjective* _____

introductory package *noun* _____

_____

_____

_____

_____

_____

Unit 15

Reading A

profile *noun* _____

temporary seasonal employee *noun* _____

loss prevention officer *noun* _____

personnel department *noun* _____

_____

_____

_____

_____

Reading B

available *adjective* _____

process *verb* _____

focus on *phrasal verb* _____

faulty *adjective* _____

overstocked *adjective* _____

leading *adjective* _____

committed *adjective* _____

promote *verb* _____

gramophone *noun* _____

_____

_____

_____

_____

Unit 16

Reading A

vacancy *noun* _____

salary *noun* _____

CV (curriculum vitae) *noun* _____

technician *noun* _____

(well) motivated *adjective* _____

applicant *noun* _____

referee *noun* _____

floor staff *noun* _____

_____

_____

_____

_____

_____

Reading B

specify *verb* _____

qualification *noun* _____

enable *verb* _____

access *noun* _____

equal opportunities *plural noun* _____

discrimination *noun* _____

marital status *noun* _____

creed *noun* _____

ethnic *adjective* _____

compulsory *adjective* _____

inaccuracy *noun* _____

falsification *noun* _____

termination *noun* _____

_____

_____

_____

_____

Appendix 2
Learning tips

Each unit of this book contains one *Learning tip*. However, this does not mean that this *Learning tip* is useful in only that particular unit. Most *Learning tips* can be used in several different units. Here are all the *Learning tips* in the book. Each one is under its unit heading and you will also find a list of the types of text you read in that unit.

When you have completed a unit, decide which text you used the *Learning tip* with (this could be more than one text type). In addition, look at the other *Learning tips* and decide if you also used any of those tips in the unit you have just finished. Make a note of the unit name and number and the text type on the empty lines. In this way, you can keep a record of the reading strategies that you are developing.

Unit 1 Is there a bank?

Learning tip

We sometimes look through a text to find a particular piece of information. This type of reading is called *scanning*. When we scan, we don't read every word. We find the information we're looking for and then stop reading. We don't pay any attention to the rest of the text.

A leaflet ☐
B notices ☐

Which other units have you used this *Learning tip* in?

Unit 2 Airmail, please!

Learning tip

We often look at a text quickly to find out what it is about or to get a general idea of its meaning. We look at pictures and headings, as well as the text itself. This type of reading is called *skimming*. When we skim, we don't read every word. We get the main idea and don't pay attention to the small details.

A leaflet ☐
B leaflet ☐

Which other units have you used this *Learning tip* in?

Unit 3 What's on?

Learning tip

When you read, it isn't necessary to understand every word in the text. You only need to understand the parts of the text which contain the information you are looking for.

A programme ☐
B leaflet ☐

Which other units have you used this *Learning tip* in?

Unit**4** What's in your luggage?

Learning tip

As you read, try to work out the meaning of unknown words. Use pictures where possible. Find other words in the text which can help you. For example, find a synonym (a word with a similar meaning to the unknown word), an antonym (a word which means the opposite), or an example. Only use a dictionary to check your guesses.

A webpage ☐
B notice ☐

Which other units have you used this *Learning tip* in?

Unit**5** Where shall we eat?

Learning tip

Our purpose in reading a text is to understand the writer's message. This means understanding the words the writer uses and also understanding what the writer wants to do with these words. They could be giving an instruction, presenting facts, giving the writer's opinion, etc. Understanding a text requires us to work out the *function* of each sentence.

A guidebook ☐
B webpage ☐

Which other units have you used this *Learning tip* in?

Unit**6** Somewhere to stay

Learning tip

Before you read a text, think about the topic – either in your own language or in English. Use your knowledge and experience to try and predict what the text – the whole text and/or parts of it – will say. You probably won't be able to predict the exact words, but it will help you understand the text if you can predict the kind of thing it will say.

A webpage ☐
B webpage ☐

Which other units have you used this *Learning tip* in?

Unit**7** On top of Table Mountain

Learning tip

When you come across an unknown word, don't stop. Continue reading and – if you think it is an important word – come back to it later. Try and work out its meaning. Decide whether the word is an adjective, noun, verb, etc. Think about similar words in your own language and similar words in English. Look for any examples which illustrate the unknown word. Look at any pictures for help. Look for a word you know within the word. Also, the context – the words around the unknown word – should help you to try and work out its meaning. Ask yourself: What could this word mean here? You might not be able to work out the exact meaning of a word, but you will probably have a good idea.

A leaflet ☐
B ticket ☐
leaflet ☐

Which other units have you used this *Learning tip* in?

Unit**8** It's ringing

Learning tip

When you read a text which compares similar things, use a chart to record the most important points for comparison. This type of note-taking helps to simplify the information in the text.

A leaflet ☐
B notice ☐

Which other units have you used this *Learning tip* in?

Unit**9** Don't worry!

Learning tip

When you read instructions, you need to identify the most important information in each sentence – this tells you what you have to do. Writers often use commas (,) to separate a word or a group of words from another word / group of words in the sentence. You can use commas to help you work out which is the most important part of the sentence.

A page from manual ☐
B leaflet ☐

Which other units have you used this *Learning tip* in?

Unit**10** What's in the news?

Learning tip

Reading for pleasure is the best way to improve your reading. It is also a wonderful way to meet new words. Identify words that are useful to you and keep a vocabulary notebook of these words. Give each page a title, e.g. *sport*, *education*, and write useful words in a list. For each word, note the meaning, the part of speech (noun, verb, etc.), anything special about its grammar or style (formal, informal, etc.) and write a sentence which is relevant to you.

A newspaper articles ☐
B newspaper article ☐

Which other units have you used this *Learning tip* in?

Unit**11** I've got to check my email

Learning tip

When you read a message that someone has sent you, always ask yourself why the person has sent you the message. Think about its main purpose before you read more carefully for the details. This will help you to understand the message more easily.

A emails ☐
B emails ☐

Which other units have you used this *Learning tip* in?

Unit **12** Is that spelt correctly?

Learning tip

Reading, as well as giving pleasure and information, has other advantages. It allows you to see how other people write and how they punctuate their work. You will also see a wide range of vocabulary – and how these words are spelt. Always make a note of the correct spelling of any useful words which you might need for your writing.

A chapter from book ☐
B sections from manuals ☐

Which other units have you used this *Learning tip* in?

Unit **13** How do I join?

Learning tip

When you read a difficult piece of text, you will need to read some words and sentences very carefully. In order to understand difficult parts of texts, it is a good idea to try and put the sentences of the text into your own words.

A webpage ☐
B leaflets ☐

Which other units have you used this *Learning tip* in?

Unit **14** At the sports centre

Learning tip

We skim some texts – reading quickly to get the general sense. We scan other texts – reading quickly to find a particular piece of information. Sometimes we can combine these two approaches to reading: skimming first to get the general sense and then scanning for a specific point.

A notices ☐
B notices ☐

Which other units have you used this *Learning tip* in?

Unit **15** I'd like to work here

Learning tip

When you are reading, you can use either a dictionary with English and your language or a dictionary which has definitions in English. The main advantage of using this second type of dictionary is that you are working in English all the time. Another benefit is they contain lots of examples of how words are used.

A webpage ☐
B webpage ☐

Which other units have you used this *Learning tip* in?

Unit **16** **Just the job!**

Learning tip

We often skim a text – look at it quickly – to find the part of the text which is most useful to us. We can then ignore the rest of the text and focus on the important part. We read the important part slowly, and we probably read some words/phrases/sentences more than once in order to understand the details.

A advertisements ☐
B application form ☐

Which other units have you used this *Learning tip* in?

Appendix 3
Using a dictionary

What kind of dictionary should I use?

If possible, you should use two dictionaries: a good bilingual dictionary (in both your own language and with English translations) and a good monolingual dictionary (English words with English definitions). A monolingual dictionary may give you more information about a word or phrase; in addition, it is a good idea for you to work in English as much as possible. The examples on these pages are from the *Cambridge Learner's Dictionary*.

What information can I find in a dictionary?

The most common reason for looking a word up in a dictionary is to find out its meaning. However, a dictionary can also give you a lot of other information about a word. *The Cambridge Learner's Dictionary*, for example, can give up to six types of information before the meaning of the word and two further types of information after it. These examples are all words from Unit 1.

1   the base form of the word

> Each entry begins with the base form of the word.

> **library** /ˈlaɪbrəri/ *noun* [C] a room or building that contains a collection of books and other written material that you can read or borrow

2   the pronunciation of the word

> These symbols show you how to say the word.

> **frequently** /ˈfriːkwəntli/ *adverb formal* often *a frequently asked question*

3   its part of speech

> This tells you what part of speech – noun, verb, adjective, etc. – a word is.

> **enjoyable** /ɪnˈdʒɔɪəbl/ *adjective* An enjoyable event or experience gives you pleasure. *We had a very enjoyable evening.*

4   any special grammatical features of the word

[C] shows that the noun is countable – but in this case the singular form is less common

possession /pə'zeʃᵊn/ *noun* **1** [C] a thing that you own [usually plural] *personal possessions* ○ *He woke up to discover that all his possessions had been stolen.* **2** [U] *formal* when you have or own something *I have* **in my possession** *a photograph which may be of interest to you.*

5   irregular past tense forms, plural nouns and comparatives/superlatives

Plurals which are not regular are shown.

o▸**bus** /bʌs/ *noun* [C] *plural* **buses** a large vehicle that carries passengers by road, usually along a fixed route *a school bus*

6   whether the word is used only in British English (UK) or American English (US)

UK means that a word is only used in British English; *US* means that a word is used only in American English.

takeaway /'teɪkəweɪ/ *UK* (*US* **takeout** /'teɪkaʊt/) *noun* [C] a meal that you buy in a restaurant but eat at home

7   the meaning of the word

gel /dʒel/ *noun* [C, U] a thick, clear, liquid substance, especially a product used to style hair **hair gel** ○ **shower gel**

The definition tells you what the word means.

8   example phrases or sentences

oven /'ʌvᵊn/ *noun* [C] a piece of kitchen equipment with a door which is used for cooking food *an electric oven* ○ *a microwave oven* ⊃ colour picture **The Kitchen** on page 2.

Examples (in *italics*) can show you how a word is used in a phrase/sentence.

9   other words this word goes with (collocations)

discount¹ /'dɪskaʊnt/ *noun* [C, U] a reduction in price *They offer a 10 percent* **discount on** *rail travel for students.*

Words in **bold** in an example show you which words are often used together.

Appendix 3 Using a dictionary

How should I use my dictionary?

1 At the top of each page in the *Cambridge Learner's Dictionary*, there is a word in **bold** black type. You can use this word to help you find the word you are looking for quickly. The word in the top left corner of the left page is the first word on this page; the word in the top right corner of the right page is the last word on this page. If you are looking for the word **withdrawn**, it will be between the two words **witch** (top left corner of the left page) and **word** (top right corner of the right page).

2 Each time you look up a word, you could use a highlighter pen to mark the word in your dictionary. When you return to a page with a highlighter mark, look at the word quickly and check that you remember its meaning.

> **mainframe** /'meɪnfreɪm/ *noun* [C] a large, powerful computer which many people can use at the same time
> **mainland** /'meɪnlənd/ *noun* **the mainland** the main part of a country, not including the islands around it *A daily ferry links the islands to the mainland.* ● **mainland** *adjective* [always before noun] *mainland Britain*
> ○ **mainly** /'meɪnli/ *adverb* mostly or to a large degree *The waitresses are mainly French.*

3 A word in your dictionary may not be exactly the same as its form in the text you are reading. This is because the word in the text may be: a verb ending in -s, -ed, -ing or an irregular form of a verb; a comparative or superlative form of an adjective e.g. *bigger*; a plural form of a noun, e.g. *children*.

> ○ **child** /tʃaɪld/ *noun* [C] *plural* **children** **1** a young person who is not yet an adult *an eight-year-old child* ○ *How many children are there in your class?* **2** someone's son or daughter, also when they are adults *Both our children have grown up and moved away.* ➔See also: **only child**.

94 **Social and travel**

4   The words that are defined in the dictionary are called
    headwords. Sometimes a headword can have more than
    one meaning. The first meaning in the dictionary is not
    always the one you want. Read through the different
    meanings and decide which one is correct in this context.

> **residential** /ˌrezɪˈdenʃ^əl/ *adjective* **1** A residen-
> tial area has only houses and not offices or fac-
> tories. **2** *UK* A residential job or course is one
> where you live at the same place as you work
> or study.

5   Words which have several meanings sometimes have a
    guideword to help you find the meaning you are looking
    for e.g. in the example below the words 'region', 'part',
    'subject' and 'size' are guidewords. Usually the most
    common meaning appears first. The first meaning in the
    dictionary is not always the one you want. Read through
    the different meanings and decide which one is correct in
    this context.

> ○•**area** /ˈeəriə/ *noun* **1** [REGION] [C] a region of a
> country or city *an industrial area* ○ *a*
> *mountainous area* ○ *the London area* **2** [PART] [C]
> a part of a building or piece of land used for a
> particular purpose *a **play**/**picnic area*** **3** [SUB-
> JECT] [C] a part of a subject or activity *Software*
> *is not really my area of expertise.* **4** [SIZE] [C, U]
> the size of a flat surface calculated by multi-
> plying its width by its length ➔See also: **catch-**
> **ment area, no-go area.**

6   Some words in your dictionary may have more than
    one headword. (Small numbers after the headword will
    indicate this.) This is because the word can be used as
    different parts of speech – for example, a verb and a noun.
    The part of speech of the unknown word should be clear
    from the context.

> ○•**hire¹** /haɪə^r/ *verb* [T] **1** *UK* (*US* **rent**) to pay money
> in order to use something for a short time
> *They hired a car for a few weeks.* ➔See Common
> learner error at **rent. 2** to begin to employ some-
> one *We hired a new secretary last week.*
> **hire sth out** *UK* to allow someone to borrow
> something from you in exchange for money
> *The shop hires out electrical equipment.*
> **hire²** /haɪə^r/ *noun* [U] *UK* when you arrange to
> use something by paying for it *The price in-*
> *cludes flights and car hire.* ○ *Do you have bikes*
> *for hire?*

When should I use my dictionary?

A dictionary is very useful when you are learning a foreign language. However, when
you are reading, do not use your dictionary too much. Using your dictionary will
interrupt your reading and slow you down. In your own language, you don't always
understand the meaning of every word; it is not necessary to understand everything
in English either.

1   When you see an English word that you do not know, first try to guess the
    meaning of the word from its context (the words around it). You may find
    another word with a similar meaning, a word which means the opposite, or
    some words which actually explain the unknown word. Only use your dictionary
    to check your guess.

2   The only other time you should look a word up in your dictionary is if there are
    no clues in the text and you are sure the unknown word is important.